CEAD ISTEACH/ENTRY PERMITTED

Cead Isteach/Entry Permitted
Nuala Ní Dhomhnaill

A collaboration between the
THE IRELAND CHAIR OF POETRY
and

UNIVERSITY COLLEGE DUBLIN PRESS
Preas Choláiste Ollscoile Bhaile Átha Cliath

2017

First published 2017
UNIVERSITY COLLEGE DUBLIN PRESS
UCD Humanities Institute
Room H103
Belfield
Dublin 4
www.ucdpress.ie

These lectures were originally published in *The Poet's Chair: The First Nine Years of the Ireland Chair of Poetry* (The Lilliput Press, 2008), and are reproduced by kind permission of the publisher.

ISBN 978-1-910820-17-9
ISSN 2009-8065 The Poet's Chair Series

CIP data available from the British Library

The right of Nuala Ní Dhomhnaill to be identified as the author of this work has been asserted by her.

Typeset in Adobe Kepler by Ryan Shiels
Text design by Lyn Davies Design
Printed in England on acid-free paper
by Antony Rowe, Chippenham, Wiltshire

Contents

vii   FOREWORD

1   Níl Cead Isteach ag an bPobal

16   Public Access Denied

33   Kismet

69   An Chailleach agus an Spéirbhean
      agus an Saol Eile i gCoitnne

95   The Hag, the Fair Maid and the
      Otherworld

121   BIOGRAPHICAL NOTE

122   ACKNOWLEDGEMENTS

123   BIBLIOGRAPHY

FOREWORD

The Trustees of the Ireland Chair of Poetry, in collaboration with UCD Press, are delighted to republish the lectures of Nuala Ní Dhomhnaill in this handsome volume. The annual lectures of the first three distinguished poets to hold the Chair, John Montague, Nuala Ní Dhomhnaill and Paul Durcan, were originally published in a joint volume, *The Poet's Chair*, by Lilliput Press in 2008. Since then, UCD Press, in the series Writings from the Ireland Chair of Poetry, has published the lectures of the three eminent poets who subsequently held the Chair: Michael Longley, Harry Clifton and Paula Meehan. This series of individual volumes is now being enhanced with the republication of the lectures of the first three professors; we are most grateful to Lilliput Press for their immediate consent and their help with this project.

The Ireland Chair of Poetry was established to honour Seamus Heaney's Nobel Prize for Literature in 1995. Modelled on the Oxford Chair of Poetry which Seamus held with grace and distinction, the Ireland Chair is a cross-border collaboration involving the two Irish Arts Councils, north and south, Queen's University Belfast, Trinity College Dublin and University College Dublin. A highlight of the professorship is the annual public lecture each professor gives and their publication constitutes an important record of the poets' engagement with their own work and that of other poets. Each of them has carried on a noble tradition of sharing their learning with new generations.

As Donnell Deeny noted in his Preface to the original publication of these lectures, Nuala Ní Dhomhnaill brought with her to the Chair "great gifts as a poet, writing brilliantly in Irish, but widely translated into English by an array of distinguished peers." In these absorbing lectures, she discusses the importance of place in Irish literature and the need to preserve important sites of Irish literary activity, writes of her initiation into Turkish life and culture and explores Ireland's rich folklore tradition.

Our sincere thanks to Mary Clayton who worked tirelessly to bring this project to fruition. I must also thank all of my other fellow Trustees, both former and currently serving, ably supported by administrator Niamh McCabe. The Ireland Chair of Poetry Trust has an assured future because of their commitment and I know that each one of them would say, with me, that it is an honour to be associated with such a visionary project.

SHEILA PRATSCHKE
Chair of the Board of Trustees, Ireland Chair of Poetry
September 2017

Níl Cead Isteach ag an bPobal
Tírdhreach Liteartha Neamhaitheanta na Gaolainne

Ba mhaith liom a shamhlú gurb é an leagan ceart Gaolainne ar an Ollúnacht seo ná Ollamh Fódla. Gabhann an t-ainm sin siar i bhfad i réimsí na staire agus na miotaseolaíochta. Deir *Leabhar Gabhála Éireann* go raibh a leithéid d'Ollamh ann. Cailleadh sa bhliain 1390 RCh é agus is in Uisneach atá sé curtha. Chreid na luathársaitheoirí chomh daingean sin sa neach miotaseolaíochta seo gur dhein Macalister tochailt ar a uaigh, más fíor. Níor thángthas ar chorp ar bith san uaigh, ar ndóigh. Níor neach ceart é an tOllamh Fódla ach neach a fáisceadh as an miotaseolaíocht. Ach ní shin le rá nach ann dó go láidir mar mheafar. Meafar ab ea é. Meafar is ea é. Is cuid de réimse miotaseolaíochta agus samhlaíochta na hÉireann é, a d'fhág a mharc ar an litríocht riamh anall, go dtí an lá inniu féin. Is gné é seo atá cosúil go maith leis an gCúigiú Cúige a mhol Mary Robinson le linn a hUachtaránachta.

Is cóir mar sin agus is ceart má tá fáil ar a uaigh in aon áit gur in Uisneach a gheofaí í, croílár tíreolaíochta agus spioradáltachta na hÉireann, lár an Chúigiú Cúige. Is é imleacán na hÉireann é, arb ionann é agus an chloch i lár shuíomh beannaithe Delphi na Gréige – *omphalos* nó imleacán an domhain. Agus go deimhin tá *omphalos* in Uisneach. Is cloch an-aisteach í go dtugann muintir na háite 'The Cat's Stone' uirthi sa Bhéarla agus go dtugtar Aill na Míreann uirthi sa Ghaolainn; glacaim leis gurb é an focal céanna é 'mír' agus 'curadhmhír', an chuid ab fhearr den fheoil go mbíodh na seanlaochra ag troid go bás ar a son. Seasann an mhír seo do chúig cúigí na hÉireann a tháinig le chéile ar an mball seo, de réir an tseanchais.

Bhí grianghraf den leacht neamhshuaithinseach seo, nach gallán, dolmain ná uaigh é, in eagrán den leabhar *Aimsir Óg* a tháinig amach le déanaí agus ina bhfuil saothar le céad scríbhneoir Gaolainne. Is maith liom a shamhlú go bhfuil cuspóir leis seo go léir. Is maith liom a shamhlú go bhfuil ceangal éigin idir céad scríbhneoir Gaolainne a bheith ann agus leac uaighe Ollamh Fódla. Fé mar a d'éirigh sé aníos ionainne. Fé mar ba sinne go léir a chuid leanaí.

Bhain go leor scríbhneoirí leas as an gcloch seo. Is cuid de chosmeolaíocht phearsanta James Joyce í. Mar sin féin, agus is pointe é seo a bheidh á dhearbhú arís agus arís eile agam sa léacht seo, is beag le rá é i gcomhthéacs an tsuímh féin in Uisneach, i gContae na hIarmhí. Tá fána bheag ann, mar is léir ón ainm Uisneach, ón nGaolainn 'uisinn'. Tugann an Duinníneach 'a temple of the head' air chun nach gceapfaí gur teampall nó foirgneamh é. Tá comhartha beag dubh is bán in aice leis agus 'Uisneach' scríofa air ach ní thugtar a thuilleadh eolais don taistealaí neamhairdiúil ná d'éinne eile a bheadh ag gabháil na slí. Cén fáth gur dóigh liom gur mór an trua é seo? Cén fáth gur dóigh liom gur sampla maith is ea é de rúnoidhreacht na hÉireann nach léir in aon chor í don ghnáthshaoránach? B'fhéidir gurb amhlaidh is fearr é. B'fhéidir gurb é an rud deireanach ar fad atá uainn ná Ionad Oidhreachta ar an suíomh seo, rud a léireodh ní arbh fhearr leat a bheith clúdaithe le tost is mistéir, ní a chaithfeadh daoine aonair a aimsiú chun go mbeadh sé ina shuíomh oilithreachta inmheánaí dóibh, mar a déarfá.

Mar b'fhéidir an rud céanna a rá fé Ráth Cruachan, tamaillín suas an bóthar i gContae Ros Comáin. An uair dheireanach a thugas cuairt ar an áit úd ní fhaca mé ach sreanganna agus feochadáin. Arís bhí comhartha beag taobh leis an ráth a dúirt go raibh cónaí anseo ar go leor de Ríthe Chonnacht. Ní luaitear Meadhbh. Ní luaitear Ailill. Ní luaitear an Táin. Ní luaitear an comhrá cáiliúil idir an bheirt agus seo sampla de le go dtuigfí cad tá i gceist:

'Is fíorbhriathar é a 'níon ó' arsa Ailill, 'is maith an bhean bean dea-fhir.'
'Is maith cheana' arsa an iníon, 'ach cén fáth duit sin a rá?'

'Tá,' arsa Ailill, 'gur fearr tusa inniu ná an lá a thógas-sa thú.'
'Ba mhaith mise romhat' arsa Meadhbh.

Agus fé mar a deir siad, 'Chuadar ón bhfocal beag go dtí an bhfocal mór le chéile':

'Cibé a imreann méala nó meirtne nó mearbhall ortsa nil éiric ná eineachlann ann duitse ach a bhfuil domsa,' arsa Meadhbh, 'mar is fear ar tionchar mná atá ionat.'

A thuilleadh maslaí sa dá threo. Ansin:

'Mar sin féin,' arsa Meadhbh, 'is mó mo mhaithsa ná do mhaithsa.' 'Is ionadh liom sin,' arsa Ailill, 'mar níl neach is mó seod agus maoin agus ollmhaitheas ná mise agus tá a fhios agam nach bhfuil.'

[O'Rahilly]

Níl aon chúlántacht anseo. Níor shuáilce í an chúlántacht i measc na Sean-Ghael, bíodh an meon athraithe ó shin nó ná bíodh.

Bhuaigh Ailill i ndeireadh na dála, go sealadach, mar is aige atá an Finnbheannach agus níl a chómhaith ag Meadhbh. Bíodh sin mar atá, tugann sí fé sheilbh a fháil ar an Donn Cuailnge, rud a chuireann tús leis an eachtra ar fad agus le téacs na Tána, an rud is cóngaraí d'eipic náisiúnta atá againn.

Nach cuma mura bhfuil macallaí na Tána le clos thart ar Ráth Cruachan mar atá sé inniu? Tar éis an tsaoil níl iontu ach scéalta. Scéalta fánacha a d'oirfeadh, mar a dúirt na manaigh féin a bhreac síos iad, *ad delectationem stultorum*, 'le haghaidh sult na n-amadán'. Ach sin é go díreach é. Níl againn ach scéalta. Insímid scéalta dá chéile le bheith beo agus chun leanúint orainn. Agus bhí suímh chomh hoiriúnach do na scéalta sin in Éirinn againn le fada an lá gur mór an trua nach féidir iad a aithint. Cuimhním agus ríméad ar leith orm ar rud éigin a thit amach nuair a bhí an dara hiníon againn, Ayse, thart ar a haon déag. An lá áirithe seo chuir sí ceist orm: 'Tás agat, a Mham, na scéalta sin go léir sa Táin – Deirdre agus Naoise agus Cú Chulainn agus an stuif sin ar fad – ar tharla sé sin go léir?' 'Bhuel is scéalta breátha iad agus fiú munar tharla siad tá siad chomh maith sin mar scéalta gur chóir gur tharla. Ach pé acu ar tharla nó nár tharla, ar a laghad ar bith tá a fhios againn an áit inar tharla siad.' 'Is cén áit ab ea é sin?' 'In Eamhain Mhacha.' 'Tá a leithéid d'áit ann mar sin?'

Agus dúrtsa go raibh a leithéid d'áit ann go deimhin agus go raibh sé ann i gcónaí – tamall lasmuigh d'Ard Mhacha i dTuaisceart Éireann – agus má bhí fonn uirthi dul ann go raghaimis ann chun é a fheiscint. Rud a dheineamar. An chéad deireadh seachtaine tar éis don tsíocháin briseadh amach, thugamar seáp ó thuaidh agus roinnt cairde inár dteannta agus bhí saol an mhadra bháin againn. Ar an mbóthar abhaile bhí an trácht go hainnis timpeall na Teorann, ach fuaireamar amach nach raibh bac ná moill orainn toisc líon mór na ndaoine a bhí amuigh agus an fonn céanna orthu is a bhí orainn féin, is é sin cuid d'Éirinn nach bhfacamar cheana, nó nach bhfacamar i gceart, a aimsiú.

Sean-nath calctha a bhaineann leis an litríocht in Éirinn ná í bheith gafa le háiteanna. Cúis mhaith ba dhóigh leat go marcálfaí na háiteanna sin ar cuid dlúth den litríocht iad. Is dócha gur i mBinn Umha gar go leor dúinne anseo, a chónaigh éinín dil na Sean-Ghaolainne, Int én bec ro léic feit, lon dubh Loch Lao.

Agus ar ndóigh cathair litearta nótáilte is ea Baile Átha Cliath. Ach i mBaile Átha Cliath féin, braithim easnamh. Gné iomlán liteartha in easnamh. Gné liteartha na Gaolainne. Sampla beag. Thuas ag Ardeaglais Naomh Pádraig tá plaic mhór tiomnaithe do na 'Writers of Dublin'. Tá scata ainmneacha luaite ann ach níl oiread is scríbhneoir Gaolainne amháin ina measc. Ba chuma liom ach an chuid seo de Bhaile Átha Cliath, go háirithe sna Libirtí taobh leis, ba nead scríbhneoireachta agus scoláireachta Gaolainne í chomh fada siar le tús an ochtú haois déag. Lárnach ann bhí an file agus an scríobhaí Seán Ó Neachtain, fear a rugadh i gContae Ros Comáin ach a bhog go Baile Átha Claith agus é ina fhear óg, áit a gcaithfeadh sé an chuid eile dá shaol. Rugadh a mhacsan, Tadhg Ó Neachtain, sa bhliain 1671. Chaith sé a shaol ar fad sna Libirtí agus áit chruinnithe a bhí sa tigh aige, ar dtús in Cole Alley, agus níos déanaí i Sráid an Iarla, ag scríbhneoirí agus scoláirí na Gaolainne, go dtí gur theip ar radharc an fhile sna 1740í. I ndán dá chuid 'Sloinfead Scothadh na Gaoidhilge Grinn' ainmníonn sé fiche is a sé scoláire Gaolainne a bhí ag saothrú leo i mBaile Átha Cliath agus máguaird. Bheadh aithne ag Déan mór na hArdeaglaise, Jonathan Swift, ar go leor acu agus chuadar i bhfeidhm air – a fhianaise sin an leagan atá aige de 'Pléaráca na Ruarcach':

Orourk's noble Fare,
　Will ne'er be forgot,
By those who were there,
　Or those who were not.

His Revels to keep,
　We sup and we dine,
On seven Score Sheep,
　Fat Bullocks and Swine.

Usquebagh to our Feast
　In Pails was brought up,
An Hundred at least,
　And a Madder our Cup.

O there is the Sport,
　We rise with the Light,
In disorderly Sort,
　From snoring all Night.

Ach an luaitear an ghníomhaíocht liteartha, agus eile, ar an bplaic atá gar d'Ardeaglais Naomh Pádraig? Faic na ngrást. Sampla eile. Ní fada ó shin ó thugas féin agus cara liom cuairt ar an teaghlach úd Bhaile na Corra, gar do Ghleann Molúra i gContae Chill Mhantáin. Is anseo a cumadh na dánta cáiliúla a fhaighimid sa *Leabhar Branach*, leabhar mhuintir Uí Bhroin. Seán Mac Airt a chuir an *Leabhar Branach* in eagar sa bhliain 1944 agus is é rud atá ann duanairí de cheithre ghlúin den teaghlach cinsealach, Gabhal Raghnaill i gContae Chill Mhantáin agus is iad na dátaí a thugann sé ná 1550 go 1630, go garbh. Seachtó trí dhán atá sa duanaire seo. Is iad sin a haon go hocht déag, Duanaire Aodha mhic Sheaáin, a naoi déag go daichead a sé, Duanaire Fhiachaidh mhic Aodha, daichead a seacht go seasca a haon, Duanaire Fheidhlim mhic Fhiachaidh, seasca a dó go seachtó a trí, Duanaire Bhriain mhic Fheidhlim. Tríocha a cúig fhile éagsúla atá sa *Leabhar Branach*. Tá cáil ar leith ar thriúr acu – Eochaidh Ó hEodhasa, Fearghal Óg Mac an Bhaird agus Tadhg Dall Ó hUiginn.

Ollamh le héigse ab ea Eochaidh Ó hEodhasa, an príomhbhard ag trí ghlúin de mhuintir Mhig Uidhir, taoisigh Fhear Manach. Duine acu, Aodh, a spreag mórdhán ar dhein James Clarence Mangan claochló air, 'O'Hussey's Ode to the Maguire'.

Ba é Tadhg Dall Ó hUiginn, a bhfuil a shaothar curtha in eagar go slachtmhar ag Eleanor Knott, an duine ab aitheanta de theaghlach na mbard úd agus ba é tuairim a chomhfhilí gurbh é ab airde orthu agus is cruthú ar a cháil líon na gcóipeanna a deineadh dá chuid lámhscríbhinní.

B'fhéidir a áiteamh gurbh é Feargal Óg Mac an Bhaird, ball de theaghlach léannta Conallach, an chéad fhile 'nua-aimseartha' sa Ghaolainn sa mhéid gur scar sé ó nósanna a chomhphroifisiúnaithe agus in áit fulaingt sa dorchadas agus cloch anuas ar a bholg – cleachtas na mbard ag an am, deirtear – thug sé fén gcumadóireacht *al fresco*, uaireanta ar muin capaill de réir dealraimh. Nó sin a chuireann Fear Flatha Ó Gnímh ina leith:

Cuimseach sin, a Fhearghail Óig,
fuarois tiodhloicthi ón Tríonóitt;
gan feidhm ndaghoide ar do dhán
ag deilbh ghlanoige ar ghearrán.

Leanann sé air:

Gan boith ndiamhoir, gan deacoir,
cead áinis as airdcheapaidh,
scor raifhérach, radharc cnoc,
amharc aiérach accat.

Ach fillimis ar an *Leabhar Branach*. Laighnigh ab ea scór de na filí a thugtar anseo. Den chuid eile, Muimhnigh ab ea triúr acu, Ultach duine eile agus Connachtaigh arís cúigear acu, ní foláir. An dá phríomh-shloinne ná Mac Eochadha agus Ó Dálaigh, baill de theaghlaigh filíochta ó Loch Garman láimh leo, agus iad ceangailte le sinsearacht mar bhaird leis na Branaigh, ach is léir go dtugadh filí fáin cuairt ar Bhaile na Corra ó thráth go chéile. Is iomaí dán molta a scríobhadh i dtaobh Bhaile na Corra. Seo ceann gairid le Donnchadh Ó Fíláin:

Beannacht ag Baile na Corra,
mo chuairt ann is aithghearr liom;
ní fhuil mo thol dún ag díorghadh
[is] dol ón dún fhíonmhar fhionn.

Baile na Corra ar gcuan sealga,
seanróimh oinigh Innsi Néill,
beag an t-iongnadh buadh 'gá bhuidhnibh
d'iolradh na sluagh suilbhir séimh.

Mo bheannacht féin fágbhuim agaibh,
a fhuil Raghnaill na reacht suairc;
bhar meadh ga héineang a n-uighinn
feadh Éireann dá gcuirinn cuairt?

[Mac Airt]

Is geal liom an focal 'sean-Róimh' mar chur síos ar an mball daoiniúil úd. Mheabhródh sé luathvéarsa duit a chuireann síos go binbeach ar Ghleann Dá Loch mar 'Róimh' i gcomparáid le hEamhain Mhacha a bhí tráth fé ghlóir. B'shin an uair go raibh an mhainistir i nGleann Dá Loch i mbarr a réime agus gan i mBaile Átha Cliath ach cúpla bothán cois Life.

Tagann an geimhreadh dian dubh agus tugaim cuairt ar Bhaile na Corra, an teaghlach úd a mbíodh fáilte roimh fhilí i gcónaí ann. Tá fonn orm féachaint ar thrí ráth nó lios a fheicim ar an Mapa Shuirbhéireacht Ordanáis i mbaile fearainn Charraig an Chróigh, an áit chéanna a luaitear sa *Leabhar Branach* de réir dealraimh:

> Iosdadh niamhghlan Cairrge an Chróigh
> nách iatar le haidhbhle sluaigh,
> Traoi Laighion an síodhmhúr séimh,
> díobhdhúdh dom chéill m'aigheadh uaidh.
>
> [Mac Airt]

Is é rud ata againn san fhocal 'cróigh' anseo ná an tuiseal ginideach den fhocal *cróch* – planda. (Táim an-tugtha do na sonraí bith-luibheolaíochta seo). Ba gheal le filí riamh an áit seo, déarfainn. Chuirtí na múrtha fáilte rompu. Tearmann ab ea é agus bia ar fáil ann, deoch, meas ar an bhfilíocht agus an saghas íocaíochta a bhí ag dul dóibh le sinsearacht, mar ba cheart – i bhfocail eile, capaill, ar a laghad, seachas ba.

Luann Eochaidh Ó hEodhasa i ndán 47 trí lios nó ráth nó feirm dhaingnithe mar chuid den áitreabh:

> Ionmhuin teach ré ttugus cúl,
> fionnbhrugh luchtmhar na lios mbán,
> múr síodhfhoirfe sliombláith saor,
> fionnráith chaomh líodhoilfe lán.
>
> [Mac Airt]

Féachaim go grinn ar an léarscáil agus ansin féachaim tharam agus mé ag iarraidh an suíomh a shamhlú dom féin. De réir a chéile aithním an príomhráth dar liom, ráth na mban agus ráth na gcuairteoirí. Tá dhá cheann acu mar chuid de chríochghort agus ceann acu leathscriosta is iad fé raon mo shúl. Más ann don cheann eile, caithfidh gur os mo chomhair amach atá sé lastall den chnoc. Is lag íseal mílítheach é solas an gheimhridh, dath an chopair is na cré-umha ar an aiteann is ar an gcíb is ar an síoda móna a bhí corcra tráth, is táim ag fiafraí díom féin an mbainfidh mé amach an ráth deireanach acu in aon chor. Ach ag bun an bhóithrín feicim comhartha a bhaineann stangadh asam – PUBLIC ACCESS DENIED. Ligim osna. Is dócha gur cheart go mbeinn sásta gurb ann dóibh i gcónaí mar ráthanna. D'fhéadfadh duine iad a leagadh le JCB i ngan fhios don saol Fódlach. Má moladh iad i ndán i ndiaidh dáin níl stádas leachtanna poiblí acu. Níl siad ar an liosta. Ritheann sé liom fiú dá mba leachtanna poiblí iad, ní bheidís saor ón loitiméireacht. Dá loitfí iad, chroithfeadh daoine a nguaillí agus bhainfí den liosta iad. Tá sé sin ag tarlúint go rábach ar fud na tíre.

Ba mhaith liom sampla a tharrac chugam anois ó Chúige Mumhan maidir leis an ngné neamhaitheanta sin de shaol na hÉireann ó thaobh litríocht na Gaolainne de. Ar an gceathrú lá de mhí Bealtaine 1773, lámhachadh Art Ó Laoghaire i gCarraig an Ime, Contae Chorcaí. Ba chaptaen óg teasaí é sna Husáir Ungáracha, é tagtha abhaile ón Mór-Roinn agus é curtha ó choimirce an dlí mar gheall ar dhrochaighneas idir é agus Abraham Morris, Ard-Sirriam Chorcaí. Bhain an t-aighneas le capall a theastaigh ó Mhorris a cheannach ó Art ar chúig phunt, mar a bhí ceadaithe dó fé na Péindlíthe a bhí i bhfeidhm ag an am. B'shin an luach ba mhó ar chapall, de réir an dlí, a cheadaítí do Chaitliceach. Ní raibh ann ach mioneachtra ag an am taobh leis an éagóir a bhí coitianta gach áit. Ní bheadh puinn eolais againn ina thaobh murach gur spreag sé ceann de na caointe is mó a scríobhadh riamh agus ceann de na dánta grá ab fhearr – 'Caoineadh Airt Uí Laoghaire', a chum a bhaintreach óg Eibhlín Dubh Ní Chonaill. Ina léacht tionscnaimh mar Ollamh le hÉigse in Oxford thug Peter Levi an dán ba mhó a scríobhadh sna hoileáin seo san ochtú haois déag air. Pé acu ar scríobhadh in aon chor é nó ar cumadh mar léiriú aithriseoireachta é nó pé acu go deimhin arbh í Eibhlín Dubh féin a chum, is ábhar mór díospóireachta ag scoláirí é sin fé láthair agus fágfaidh mé fúthu é. Ach is ann don dán agus seo chugaibh a thús le go mbraithfidh sibh an bheogacht agus an dobrón atá ann agus an chuisle dhúchasach:

Mo ghrá go daingean tu!
Lá dá bhfaca thu
Ag ceann tí an mhargaidh,
Thug mo shúil aire dhuit,
Thug mo chroí taitneamh duit,
D'éalaíos óm charaid leat
I bhfad ó bhaile leat.

Is domhsa nárbh aithreach:
Chuiris parlús á ghealadh dhom
Rúmanna á mbreacadh dhom,
Bácús á dheargadh dhom,
Brící á gceapadh dhom,
Rósta ar bhearaibh dom,
Mairt á leagadh dhom;
Codladh i gclúmh lachan dom
Go dtíodh an t-eadartha
Nó thairis dá dtaitneadh liom.

[Ó Tuama]

Is ann i gcónaí i Maigh Chromtha do 'cheann tí an mhargaidh' agus aon uair go mbím ag dul thar bráid an aon iontas é go mbíonn an dán mór seo á aithris agam dom féin os íseal? Anuas air sin, suíomh seo an ghrá chomhlíonta a gcuireann Eibhlín Dubh síos air, is ann dó i gcónaí i dtigh Airt Uí Laoghaire i Ráth Laoich, gar do Mhaigh Chromtha. Nuair a thosnaíos ar an léacht seo a bhreacadh síos bhí Tigh Ráth Laoich ar díol agus bhí cás á dhéanamh ag scoláirí agus ag scríbhneoirí go gceannódh an Stát é. Theastaigh ionad cultúrtha uathu anseo a d'fhreastalódh ar leas an chultúir dhátheangaigh agus ar leas na n-ealaíon scríofa agus léiriúcháin. D'fhéadfadh an tigh a bheith ina thearmann spioradálta, ina áit chruinnithe, ina thearmann do scríbhneoirí, ina leabharlann, ina ionad acmhainní, ina amharclann agus mar sin de. Is geata isteach i Múscraí Thiar é ina bhfuil an dá theanga fós á labhairt agus á gcanadh. Tháinig seanchaithe iontacha chun cinn i Múscraí Thiar – scéalaithe i nGaolainn agus i mBéarla – Amhlaoibh Ó Loingsigh a cailleadh i 1947 agus Tadhg Ó Buachalla, an táilliúir cáiliúil in *The Tailor and Ansty*. Is ann a tháinig chun cinn amhránaithe móra dátheangacha ar nós Bess Cronin, gan trácht ar Chór Chúil Aodha a bhunaigh Seán Ó Riada, duine de na chéad daoine a d'aithin saibhreas cultúrtha na háite. Áitíodh gurb é an chúis ar caomhnaíodh an tigh réamh-Sheoirseach agus an clós stábla mór daingnithe cloiche ná an meas a bhí ag na húinéirí i gcaitheamh na mblianta, i dteannta an phobail áitiúil, ar shuíomh 'Chaoineadh Airt Uí Laoghaire'. Deir Máirín Ní Dhonnchadha ó Ollscoil na Gaillimhe go bhfuil an tigh '... salvific in itself and can also stand for the good that poetry effects in people's lives when it is shared with them'.

Is é an caoineadh seo, a deir sí, 'ag Eibhlín Ní Chonaill an dán is aitheanta ó thraidisiún Gaelach an ochtú haois déag, nó go deimhin ó litríocht na Gaeilge trí chéile roimh an bhfichiú haois agus ar fud an domhain. Ach bhí stádas éiginnte aige san am ar cumadh é nuair ba mhó an meas a bhí ar fhoirmeacha ardstílithe filíochta ná ar an dán paiseanta a tháinig amach ón gcroí. Dá réir sin seasann 'Caoineadh Airt Uí Laoghaire' do ghnéithe dár n-oidhreacht atá fós le haimsiú agus le luacháil agus le hathluacháil lenár linn féin.

Luadh tábhacht an cheantair chomh maith i gcomhthéacs dhá fhoirm lárnacha de litríocht Ghaolainne an ochtú haois déag – an barántas agus an aisling. Sa cheantar seo a rugadh beirt de mhórscríbhneoirí Gaolainne na haoise sin – Aogán Ó Rathaille agus Eoghan Rua Ó Súilleabháin. Luadh leanúnachas an traidisiún i Múscraí Thiar, mar shampla an mórfhile pobail Máire Bhuí Ní Laoghaire a rugadh anseo i 1771, bliain i ndiaidh bhás Airt Uí Laoghaire. Rugadh an scríbhneoir agus an t-athbheochantóir an tAthair Peadar Ua Laoghaire i bparóiste Chluain Droichead, nach bhfuil rófhada ón áit, deich mbliana sular cailleadh Máire, agus rugadh Seán Ó Ríordáin, an file Gaolainne ab

fhearr sa chéad leath den fhichiú haois, rugadh eisean i mBaile Bhuirne
tamall de bhlianta tar éis bhás an Athar Peadar.

Ba mhún in aghaidh na gaoithe é. Tháinig litir ó rúnaí príobháideach
Shíle de Valera, a bhí ag an am sin ina hAire Ealaíon, Oidhreachta,
Gaeltachta agus Oileán, nach ndúirt ach go raibh Tigh Ráth Laoich ar
thaifid na struchtúr cosanta ag Comhairle Chontae Chorcaí agus go
raibh Tigh Thraolaigh i gCaisleán an Bharraigh, Contae Mhaigh Eo,
chun ligint don Ard-Mhúsaem bailiúchán de lámhdhéantúsáin tíre a
thaispeáint i dtimpeallacht oiriúnach, agus go bunúsach go raibh an
oidhreacht ailtireachta á cosaint ag na hAchtanna Pleanála. Brilléis!
Cén bhaint atá ag Maigh Eo le litríocht na Mumhan? Mar Mhuimhneach
mé féin – (mheasas gur Éireannach a bhí ionam go dtí gur chuas chun
cónaithe i mBaile Átha Cliath agus mé i lár na dtríochaidí agus gur
tuigeadh dom gur sa Pháil a bhíos agus go dtí sin nár chónaíos in aon
áit in Éirinn lasmuigh de Chúige Mumhan) – faighim an-bhlas ar línte
deireanacha Chaoineadh Eibhlín Dubh.

> Mo ghrá thu agus mo rún!
> Tá do stácaí ar a mbonn,
> Tá do bha buí á gcrú;
> Is ar mo chroí atá do chumha
> Ná leigheasfadh Cúige Mumhan
> Ná Gaibhne Oileáin na bhFionn.

> [Ó Tuama]

An tábhacht a bhaineann leis an litríocht ina suíomh nádúrtha, ba
phointe é sin a chuaigh amú ar an aire.

An sampla deireanach a theastaíonn uaim a thabhairt anseo de
litríocht na Gaolainne i suíomh nádúrtha, is sampla é atá níos cóngaraí
dúinn anseo i mBéal Feirste agus le bheith féaráilte ní sampla diúltach
é. Baineann sé le hoidhreacht liteartha Oirialla mar a thugann an
tOllamh Breandán Ó Buachalla uirthi, is é sin Ulaidh Thoir Theas. De
thairbhe an obair cheannródaíoch a dhein an Cairdinéal Tomás Ó
Fiaich, nach maireann, agus é ina Ollamh le Nua-Ghaeilge i gColáiste

Mhaigh Nuad, aithnítear an chuid seo de Chúige Uladh ar cheann de phríomhcheantair na gníomhaíochta liteartha Gaolainne iarchlasaicí sa tír seo. Agus tús curtha leis ag Séamas Dall Mac Cuarta (1647–1733) agus fad le hArt Mac Bionaid agus Art Mac Cumhaigh, tháinig seoda chun cinn ón gcultúr sin i gcaitheamh tréimhse neamhbhriste de bhlianta fada. Áirítear anseo forbairt ar mheadaracht nua, trí rainn agus amhrán, is é sin le rá trí véarsa ghearra a bhí bunaithe ar mheadarachtaí fhilíocht na mBard agus véarsa deiridh bunaithe ar mheadaracht aiceanta na n-amhrán. I measc na saothar iontach caithfear 'Úr-Chill an Chreagáin' a lua mar cheann de na móraislingí i stair an tseánra trí chéile. Tá binneas thar na beartaibh ann agus mairfidh sé fad a mhairfidh an Ghaolainn. (Tá leagan luathchlóite den téacs againn a d'fhoilsigh an scríobhaí Nioclás Ó Cearnaigh i dtuairiscí an Chumainn Oisínigh):

Ag Úr-Chill an Chreagáin chodail mé aréir faoi bhrón,
is le héirí na maidne tháinig ainnir fá mo dhéin le póig,
bhí gríosghrua ghartha aici agus loinnir ina céibh mar ór,
is gurbh é íocshláinte an domhain bheith ag amharc ar an ríoghain óig.

[Ó Buachalla]

Glaonn an tsí-bhean air chun domhan seo an dóláis a thréigint agus tar éis a bheith siar agus aniar léi diúltaíonn sé don chuireadh agus fógraíonn gur mian leis bheith curtha san áit ina bhfuil sé anois i reilig an Chreagáin:

má éagaim fán tSeanainn, i gcrích Mhanainn, nó san Éiphte mhór,
gurb ag Gaeil chumhra an Chreagáin a leagfar mé i gcré faoi fhód.

[Ó Buachalla]

Is ábhar sóláis dúinn a fháil amach gur fíoradh guí paiseanta an fhile. Sa reilig shlachtmhar taobh le hEaglais na hÉireann sa Chreagán tá leac uaighe ann a thaispeánann dúinn cá bhfuil Art Mac Cumhaigh curtha. Lastall den bhalla íseal tá abhainn agus lúb leathan inti. An uair dheireanach a bhíos ann bhí an ghaoth ag siosarnach i measc na gcrann, an t-uisce ag spraoi i lúb na habhann agus bhí séimhe ar fud na háite a chuir le mo thuiscint do bhua na hinspioráide a bhi laistiar den dán 'Úr-Chill an Chreagáin'. Níos spéisiúla fós, is ann atá Néilligh an Fheadha agus a thuilleadh den treibh chéanna. Fuarthas é seo amach trí thimpiste nuair a bhí athnuachan á déanamh ar an reilig, gur ghabh meaisín tochailte isteach i bpoll mór sa talamh. Nach spéisiúil le samhlú é go mbeadh Art Mac Cumhaigh i bhfolach sa tuama céanna agus cnámha mhuintir Néill thart air nuair a scríobh sé na focail seo:

Is é mo ghéarghoin tinnis gur theastaigh uainn Gaeil Thír Eoghain,
agus oidhríbh an Fheadha, gan seaghais faoi léig 'ár gcomhair,
géagaibh glandaite Néill Fhrasaigh nachar dhiúlt do cheol,
chuirfeadh éide fá Nollaig ar na hollaimh bheadh ag géilleadh
dóibh.

[Ó Buachalla]

Domsa agus do go leor daoine eile chomh maith, déarfainn, b'ionann teacht ar thuama na Néilleach mar sin agus tuama Thútancámúin á oscailt. Tuigim go binn conas a scríobhadh dán ina bhfuil sárliriciúlacht agus an-áilleacht chaointeach in áit mar seo. Cuireann sé scéal i gcuimhne dom a d'inis Mícheál Ó hAirtnéide dom tráth. De réir dealraimh, nuair a bhíodh corp na bhFarónna á n-aistriú i mbád óna dtuamaí síos feadh na Níle, leanadh muintir na háite, na *fellahin*, iad feadh dhá bhruach na habhann agus iad ag caoineadh is ag béicíl is ag scréachaíl ar feadh i bhfad i ndiaidh na ríthe a bhí orthu tráth. Domsa mar sin is sampla den iontas agus den draíocht í reilig an Chreagáin a thugann an traidisiún liteartha áitiúil dúinn ach beagán cúraim a ghlacadh leis.

Tagann dánta as gach aon áit. As an aigéan gorm agus as an spéir i bhfad uainn. Dá mbeadh a fhios agam cad is ábhar dáin ann chuirfinn i mbuidéal agus dhíolfainn é. Ach tá a fhios agam rud amháin go cinnte – gineann dánta dánta eile. Gineann scéalta agus amhráin tuilleadh scéalta. Tagann athrú ar an bhfoirm, ar an teanga is ar an seánra ach dá mhéad dá n-athinsítear iad is ea is mó a chuireann siad le pléisiúr iomlán agus sonas an duine.

Dá réir sin, is den tábhacht é ná deinimis dearmad ar an ngníomhaíocht liteartha *in situ* agus tá súil agam go mbeidh ardmheas ar na céadta bliain de ghníomhaíocht liteartha na Gaolainne mar ghné shuaithinseach de chultúr an phobail agus nach bhfágfar fé shainghrúpaí scolártha amháin í. Tá sé tábhachtach mar sin go n-éileofaí saorchead isteach ag cách sa traidisiún sin, ar ais nó ar éigean.

Tras-scríbhinn de léacht a tugadh in Ollscoil na Banríona, Béal Feirste, i mí na Nollag 2001.

Public Access Denied
or the Unrecognised Literary Landscape of Irish

I would like to think that the proper Irish translation of the Ireland Chair of Poetry is 'Ollamh Fódla'. This is a name that goes back a long way and stretches into the distant reaches of history and mythology. According to *Leabhar Gabhála Éireann* (*The Book of Invasions*), there was an Ollamh Fódla. He died way back in 1390 BC and is buried at Uisneach. Early antiquaries believed so implicitly in this obviously mythological entity that Macalister excavated his reputed grave. Of course, no body was found in the grave. Ollamh Fódla was never a real person, in that he was a mythological entity. But that doesn't make him any less real in metaphoric terms. He was a metaphor. He is a metaphor. He is a marker of a mythological and imaginative dimension of Irish life that has been expressed since time immemorial in literature, and as such is being readily expressed today. This is a dimension akin to that Fifth Province espoused by Mary Robinson during her presidency.

It is therefore apt that if his reputed grave is anywhere, it should be at Uisneach, the geographical and spiritual dead centre of Ireland, the centre of the Fifth Province, the *imleacán*, or bellybutton, of Ireland, equivalent to the stone at the centre of the sacred site of Delphi in Greece – the *omphalos*, or navel, of the world. And there is an *omphalos* in Uisneach. A distinctly weird-looking stone, locally called The Cat's Stone in English, and known in Irish as *Aill na Míreann*; *mír* being probably the same word as in *curadhmhír*, the champion's portion, which the ancient warriors were wont to fight about to the death. This portion refers to the five divisions of Ireland that supposedly come together at that spot.

A photograph of this unprepossessing monument, neither a *gallán* (standing stone), dolmen nor grave, appeared in a recent edition of *Aimsir Óg*, a book containing the work of one hundred Irish-language writers. I like to think it is there for a purpose, that the possibility exists of at least a hundred writers in modern Irish who are somehow connected with the gravestone of Ollamh Fódla. As if it were resurrected in us. As if we were somehow all his children.

This Cat's Stone has been important for many writers. It is a part of the personal cosmology of James Joyce. Nevertheless, and this is the point I will be making again and again in this lecture, it would be very hard to make anything of it on the actual site of Uisneach itself, in County Westmeath. The site has a slight gradient, as implied by its name, Uisneach, from the Irish *uisinn* or temple. Ó Duinnín calls this 'a temple of the head', no doubt to distinguish it from a temple which might be a building or edifice. There is a small black-and-white sign nearby marking it as 'Uisneach', but no extra information is given to the unwary traveller, or to anybody else who might come that way. Why do I think this is a pity? Why do I think that it is typical of the deeply coded heritage of Ireland, which is well-nigh invisible to the ordinary citizen? Maybe it is better so. Maybe the last thing on earth we want is a Heritage Centre on the site, making blatantly obvious what is best left half in mystery and silence, to be searched out by individuals, making it, as it were, a site of inner pilgrimage.

The same could be said for Ráth Cruachan, just slightly up the road in County Roscommon. On my last visit to the site there was nothing to see except razor wire and thistles. Again, a small sign beside the rath notes only that this was the dwelling place of many of the kings of Connaught. No Meadhbh. No Ailill. No mention of the Táin. No pillow talk. Here are a few snippets of the very same pillow talk (translation from the Táin by Thomas Kinsella) by way of showing what is at stake:

'It is true what they say, love,' Ailill said, 'it is well for the wife of a wealthy man.'
'True enough,' the woman said. 'What put that in your mind?'

'It struck me,' Ailill said, 'how much better off you are today than the day I married you.'

'I was well enough off without you,' Meadhbh said.

And as they say in Irish, '*Chuadar ón bhfocal beag go dtí an bhfocal mór le chéile*', which you could translate as saying, 'They started out with the small insults and went on to the big insults with each other':

'So if anyone causes you shame or upset or trouble, the right to compensation is mine,' Meadhbh said, 'for you're a kept man.'

More insults each way. Then:

'It still remains,' Meadhbh said, 'that my fortune is greater than yours.'

'You amaze me,' Ailill said. 'No one has more property or jewels or precious things than I have.'

No false modesty here. The like was never considered a virtue in Old Irish; however mores may have changed in the meantime.

They end up with Ailill winning, temporarily, because he has the *Finnbheannach*, or white-horned bull, and Meadhbh doesn't have its equivalent. Undaunted, she sets out to get possession of the brown bull of Cooley, creating a pretext for the whole adventure of the *Táin*, the nearest we have to a national epic.

Why should it matter that the echoes of the *Táin* are not heard around modern Ráth Cruachan? After all they are nothing but stories, idle tales, suitable, as noted by the very monks who wrote them down, *ad delectationem stultorum*, 'for the amusement of idiots'. But that is my very point. Stories are all we have. Stories are what we tell each other to keep going, to keep alive. And in Ireland we have had such a suitable setting for these stories for so long that it is a pity not to recognise it. I remember with particular joy something that happened when my second daughter, Ayse, was about eleven. She came to me one day with a question: 'You know, Mam, those stories about the *Táin* – Deirdre and Naoise and Cuchulainn and all that stuff? Did it really happen?' 'Well, they are very good stories, and even if they didn't happen they are such good stories that they should have happened. But whether they happened or not, at least we know where they happened.' 'And where was that?' 'At Eamhain Mhacha.' 'Is that really a place then?'

And it was with great aplomb that I insisted that yes, indeed it was a place and that is was still there – Navan Fort, just outside Armagh in Northern Ireland, and that if she wanted we could go and see it. And we did. The first weekend that peace broke out we made a jaunt with some friends to Armagh and parts north and had the time of our lives. On the way home the traffic around the border was dreadful, but we discovered that there were no hold-ups, or slow-downs, or checkpoints involved. It was due to the sheer number of people who had had the same idea as ourselves, and were out to discover a hitherto not so well-known part of Ireland.

One of the timeworn clichés about literature in Ireland is that it is very much a literature of place. All the more reason, one would think, that we should mark the actual places that are so much a part of the literature. Cavehill, just beside us here in Belfast, is more than likely the dwelling of the first beloved bird of Old Irish, *Int én bec ro léic feit*, the blackbird of Loch Lao.

And Dublin of course is a noted literary city. But in Dublin itself, I notice an absence. A loss of a whole literary dimension. The literary dimension of the Irish language. A small example: up by St Patrick's Cathedral there is a large plaque dedicated to the 'Writers of Dublin'. It gives many names but not one single Irish-language writer is mentioned. I wouldn't mind, but this particular area of Dublin, especially the nearby Liberties, was a veritable hotbed of Irish writing and scholarship going back as far as the start of the eighteenth century. It centered on the poet and scribe Seán Ó Neachtain who, though born in County Roscommon, moved to Dublin as a young man and spent the rest of his life there. His son, Tadhg Ó Neachtain, born in 1671, lived all his life in the Liberties and his houses, first at Cole Alley, and later in Earl Street, were meeting places for Irish writers and scholars until his sight failed in the 1740s. His poem, 'Sloinfead Scothadh na Gaoidhilge Grinn' ('I Will Name the Best of Clear Irish'), names twenty-six Gaelic scholars working in Dublin and thereabouts. Many of them would have been familiars of the great Dean of St Patrick's, Jonathan Swift, who profited from them, if his version of 'Pléaráca na Ruarcach' ('O Rourke's Ructions') is anything to go by:

Orourk's noble Fare,
  Will ne'er be forgot,
By those who were there,
  Or those who were not.

His Revels to keep,
  We sup and we dine,
On seven Score Sheep,
  Fat Bullocks and Swine.

Usquebagh to our Feast
  In Pails was brought up,
An Hundred at least,
  And a Madder our Cup.

O there is the Sport,
  We rise with the Light,
In disorderly Sort,
  From snoring all Night.

But is there any mention of all this literary and other activity on the plaque near St Patrick's Cathedral? Devil the whit. To give another example, not so long ago a friend and I visited the site of the household of Ballinacor, near Glenmalure in County Wicklow. This is where the famous poems that make up the *Leabhar Branach* (*Book of the O'Byrnes*) were composed. The *Leabhar Branach*, edited by Seán Mac Airt in 1944, comprises the poem books of four generations of the ruling family of Gabhal Raghnaill in County Wicklow, and he dates them from the period between roughly 1550 and 1630. There are seventy-three poems in this *Duanaire*, or poem book. These are made up of one to eighteen, the *Duanaire* of Aodh Mac Seáin, nineteen to forty-six, the *Duanaire* of Fiach Mac Aoidh, forty-seven to sixty-one, the *Duanaire* of Fheidhlim Mac Aoidh, and sixty-two to seventy-three, the *Duanaire* of Brian Mac Fheidhlim. In all some thirty-five different poets are represented in the *Leabhar Branach*. Three of these are particularly well known – Eochaidh Ó hEodhasa, Fearghal Óg Mac an Bhaird, and Tadhg Dall Ó hUiginn.

Eochaidh Ó hEodhasa was *ollamh* or chief poet to three successive heads of the Maguires, chieftains of Fermanagh, of which one, Aodh, inspired a great poem, which was transmogrified by James Clarence Mangan into 'O'Hussey's Ode to the Maguire'.

Tadhg Dall Ó hUiginn, whose work has been so eminently edited by Eleanor Knott, was the best-known member of the Ó hUiginn bardic family and was considered by many other poets as absolutely outstanding in his time – the sheer amount of manuscript copies of his work attests to this fame.

Fearghal Óg Mac an Bhaird, a member of a famous learned Donegal family, could by some rights be called the first 'modern' poet in Irish, in that he supposedly broke ranks with his fellow professionals. Instead of suffering in the dark with a stone on his belly, as was supposedly the bardic practice at the time, he took to composing *al fresco*, sometimes reputedly on horseback. Or so he is charged by Fear Flatha Ó Gnímh:

Cuimseach sin, a Fhearghail Óig,
fuarois tiodhloicthi ón Tríonóitt;
gan feidhm ndaghoide ar do dhán
ag deilbh ghlanoige ar ghearrán.

This was translated by Osborn Bergin as:

This is comfortable, O Fearghal Óg,
Thou has gotten gifts from the Trinity:
Without any need of a good teacher for thy verse
Thou framest fine scholarly art on horseback.

He goes on:

> Gan boith ndiamhoir, gan deacoir,
> cead áinis as airdcheapaidh,
> scor raifhérach, radharc cnoc,
> amharc aiérach accat.

> Without a dark hut, without hardship,
> With leave to take delight in lofty invention,
> A grassy scaur, a view of mountains,
> An airy prospect are thine.

But to return to the *Leabhar Branach*, twenty of the poets arrayed here have been identified as Leinster poets. Of the remainder, three are probably from Munster, one from Ulster, and five probably from Connaught. The two main surnames are Mac Eochadha (anglicised as McKeogh) and Ó Dálaigh, members of two poetic families from nearby Wexford, who were attached to the O'Byrnes as hereditary bards, but it is evident that many other wandering poets visited Ballinacor from time to time.

Many poems were written in praise of Ballinacor. Here is a short one by Donnchadh Ó Fíláin:

> Beannacht ag Baile na Corra,
> mo chuairt ann is aithghearr liom;
> ní fhuil mo thol dún ag díorghadh
> [is] dol ón dún fhíonmhar fhionn.

> Baile na Corra ar gcuan sealga,
> seanróimh oinigh Innsi Néill,
> beag an t-iongnadh buadh 'gá bhuidhnibh
> d'iolradh na sluagh suilbhir séimh.

> Mo bheannacht féin fágbhuim agaibh,
> a fhuil Raghnaill na reacht suairc;

bhar meadh ga héineang a n-uighinn
feadh Éireann dá gcuirinn cuairt?

My fond farewell to Ballinacor.
My visit there seems much too short for me.
My heart is not happy
Leaving that bright hall full of wine.

Ballinacor of the hunting lodges
An ancient Rome on O'Neill's isle.
It was small wonder to be without worry
In the multiplicity of its merry, happy crowds.

I leave you with all my blessing
People of Clann Raghnaill of the pleasant rule.
It is a great loss for me to leave you
Though I visit all the length and breadth of Ireland.

[Mac Airt]

I especially like the word *seanróimh* – the 'Ancient Rome' that is used to describe the populous quarters. This reminds me of an early verse that rather vengefully calls Glendalough a *ruam* or 'Rome' compared with the erstwhile glories of Eamhain Mhacha. This from a time when the monastery of the Valley of the Two Lakes was a hive of human activity, while Dublin was still a barely identified ford of hurdles on the River Liffey.

In the slanting, early winter light I visit what can be safely identified as the once poet-welcoming household of Ballinacor. I especially want to check out what appear on the Ordnance Survey Map as three otherwise unmarked *liosanna* (raths or fortified farmhouses) in the townland of Carrigroe, which would seem to be the Cairrgre an Chróigh mentioned in the *Leabhar Branach*:

Iosdadh niamhghlan Cairrge an Chróigh
nách iatar le haidhbhle sluaigh,

Traoi Laighion an síodhmhúr séimh,
díobhdhúdh dom chéill m'aigheadh uaidh.

Carrigroe a house made of shining osiers.
A dwelling place of strength and ease
A fortress for people in this sublunary world.
A foremost example of fondness and peace.

[Mac Airt]

Here *cróigh* is the genitive of *cróch*, a saffron plant. (This is the king of bio-botanical detail for which I am an absolute sucker.) It was obviously a place beloved of poets. A house where they were always welcome. A haven where they could be sure of food, drink, respect, and the kind of payment for their poems which for centuries they had considered their due – in other words, at least horses, not cows.

Eochaidh Ó hEodhasa, in poem forty-seven, mentions the three *liosanna* that were part of the premises:

Ionmhuin teach ré ttugus cúl,
fionnbhrugh luchtmhar na lios mbán,
múr síodhfhoirfe sliombláith saor,
fionnráith chaomh líodhoilfe lán.

Beloved house on which I must turn my back.
Abundant hostel of the white raths.
Rampart without drawbacks, free with flowers
White rath full of happiness.

[Mac Airt]

I look carefully at the map, and then I look around again and try to position myself in the countryside. Gradually I begin to make out what may have been the main rath, the rath of the women and the rath of the visitors. Two of these, one half-destroyed and incorporated into a field boundary, are within sight. The other still exists, just up over the hill in front of me. In the wan, low, wintry light, with the nearby hill copper and bronze from dying bracken and sedge and the once purple moor grass, I wonder if I can make it up to see the last of the three raths. But at the foot of the *boreen* a sign stops me dead in my tracks – PUBLIC ACCESS DENIED. I sigh. I suppose I should be pleased that the raths are still there at all. At any moment someone could take a JCB to them and no one would be any the wiser. For all their praise in poem after poem, they have no public monument status. They are not listed properties. It dawns on me that even if they were public monuments, it would not help them much against wanton destruction. If they were to be destroyed, people would just shrug and promptly 'de-list' them. That is what is happening wholesale throughout the country.

Now I want to give an example from Munster of the unrecognised Irish-language literature-based dimension of Irish life. On 4 May 1773 Art Ó Laoghaire, a young hot-blooded captain in the Hungarian Hussars, back from service on the continent and outlawed because of a bitter quarrel with Abraham Morris, the High Sheriff of Cork, was shot at Carraig an Ime, County Cork. The quarrel was over a horse, which Morris, according to the penal laws in force at the time, wanted to buy from Ó Laoghaire for five pounds. This was the maximum value of a horse that a Catholic could own, according to the law. The event was to everyone except the immediate victims a more-or-less minor episode in a time of much more serious injustices. We would probably not know anything much about it, were it not for the fact that it became the occasion of one of the great laments and also love poems of all time – 'Caoineadh Airt Uí Laoghaire', the 'Lament for Art O'Leary', composed by his young widow, Eibhlín Dubh Ní Chonaill. Peter Levi, in his inaugural Oxford lecture as Professor of Poetry, calls it the greatest poem written on these islands in the eighteenth century. Whether it was actually written at all, or was composed basically as an oral performance; whether, indeed, it was actually composed by Eibhlín Dubh herself – these are all moot points, and a source of major contention to many great scholars at the moment, and I will not deem to point my toe where angels fear to tread. But it does exist, and let me quote a little from its beginning to give a feel of its vivacity, intense grief, and remarkable immediacy and verve:

Mo ghrá go daingean tu!
Lá dá bhfaca thu
Ag ceann tí an mhargaidh,
Thug mo shúil aire dhuit,
Thug mo chroí taitneamh duit,
D'éalaíos óm charaid leat
I bhfad ó bhaile leat.

Is domhsa nárbh aithreach:
Chuiris parlús á ghealadh dhom
Rúmanna á mbreacadh dhom,
Bácús á dheargadh dhom,
Brící á gceapadh dhom,
Rósta ar bhearaibh dom,
Mairt á leagadh dhom;
Codladh i gclúmh lachan dom
Go dtíodh an t-eadartha
Nó thairis dá dtaitneadh liom.

[Ó Tuama]

Here the translation is from *A Celtic Miscellany* by Kenneth Jackson:

My steadfastly beloved, on the day that I saw you beside the market-hall, my eye gave heed to you, my heart gave love to you; I stole away from my family with you, far from home with you.

Nor did I repent it. You gave me a parlour brightened for me, rooms decorated for me, the oven heated for me, loaves made for me, roast meat on spits for me, beeves butchered for me, sleep on duck's feathers for me until high morning, or later if I chose.

The *ceann tí an mhargaidh* or market-house gable mentioned here is still a noted landmark in the middle of Macroom and every time I pass it, I start murmuring parts of this great poem to myself. More to the point, the site of such nuptial bliss described by Eibhlín Dubh is still extant in Art Ó Laoghaire's house in Rathleigh, near Macroom. Around the time I was originally writing this lecture, Rathleigh House was up for sale, and a group of scholars and writers were making a case for it to be bought by the state. The case was that a cultural centre based here would have a justified claim in serving the interests of a dual-language culture and also of the performing and written arts. The house could well be a spiritual home, a meeting place, a writers' retreat, a library, a resource centre, a theatre, and much else besides. It is the gate to West Muskerry, where two languages and two literatures are still spoken and sung. West Muskerry has produced amazing *sean-chaithe* – storytellers – in Irish and English: Amhlaoibh Ó Loingsigh, who died in 1947, and Tim Buckley, the famous tailor of *The Tailor and Ansty*, as well as great dual-language folk singers such as Bess Cronin, and the Cúil Aodha Choir, founded by Seán Ó Riada, who was one of the first people to recognise the particular cultural richness of the area. It was argued that the reason the pre-Georgian house and extensive fortified stone-built stable yard had been conserved was largely because of the respect of the successive owners and also of the local community for the setting of 'Caoineadh Airt Uí Laoghaire'. As the pamphlet circulating at the time states: '[The house was] ... salvific in itself and can also stand for the good that poetry effects in people's lives when it is shared with them.'

Eibhlín Ní Chonaill's *caoineadh* is the best-known poem from the eighteenth-century Gaelic tradition, perhaps from all of pre-twentieth-century Gaelic literature in Ireland and beyond. Yet it had a more ambiguous status in its contemporary culture, some of whose brokers placed less value on passionate, spontaneous expression than on highly stylised forms of poetry. Consequently, 'Caoineadh Airt Uí Laoghaire' is well placed to symbolise what is yet to be discovered from our heritage, how we evaluate and re-evaluate it in our own time.

Appeals were made for the importance of West Muskerry with regard to two vital forms of Gaelic literature in the eighteenth century – the *barántas* and the *aisling* – and that the area was home to two of the greatest Irish writers of that century, Aogán Ó Rathaille and Eoghan Rua Ó Súilleabháin. The continuity of tradition in West Muskerry was singled out – for example, the outstanding folk poet Máire Bhuí Ní Laoghaire was born here in 1771, the year after Art Ó Laoghaire's death. The writer and language activist an tAthair Peadar Ua Laoghaire was born nearby in Clondrohid parish, some ten years before her death, and Seán Ó Ríordáin, Ireland's best Gaelic poet in the first half of the twentieth century, was born in Baile Bhuirne a few years after an tAthair Peadar's death.

The appeals fell on deaf ears. A letter from the private secretary of Síle de Valera, then Minister for the Arts, Heritage, Gaeltacht and the Islands, stated only that Ráth Laoich House was on Cork County Council's record of protected structures, that Turlough House in Castlebar, County Mayo, was being developed to allow the National Museum to put on display a collection of folkloric artefacts in a suitable setting, and that basically the architectural heritage was being protected through the planning acts. I think that was fudging the point, to put it mildly. Where is Mayo when you are talking about the literature of Munster? As a Munster woman myself – I thought I was Irish until I went to live in Dublin in my mid-thirties and realised it was beyond the Pale – I identify deeply with the last lines of Eibhlín Dubh's lament:

Mo ghrá thu agus mo rún!
Tá do stácaí ar a mbonn,
Tá do bha buí á gcrú;
Is ar mo chroí atá do chumha
Ná leigheasfadh Cúige Mumhan
Ná Gaibhne Oileáin na bhFionn.

My love and my beloved!
Your corn-stacks are standing,
your yellow cows milking,
And on my heart there is a grief for you

That the whole wide province of Munster could not cure
Nor all the craftsmen of all of Ireland.

[Ó Tuama]

The importance of literature in its natural setting, obviously the whole point of the exercise, was entirely lost on the minister.

The last example of Irish-language literature in its natural setting I would like to give is one closer to us here in Belfast. And to be fair, it is not a negative example. It concerns the literary legacy of Oirialla, or south-east Ulster, as it has been called by Professor Breandán Ó Buachalla. Largely because of the pioneering work done by the late Cardinal Tomás Ó Fiaich when he was Professor of Modern Irish at Maynooth College, this area of Ulster has now been recognised for what it is, as one of the main areas of post-classical Gaelic literary activity in the country. Starting with Séamas Dall Mac Cuarta and lasting up to Art Mac Bionaid and Art Mac Cumhaigh, the unbroken years have yielded the culture many felicities. These include the development of a metrical form – *trí rainn agus amhrán* – three short stanzas based on the metres of the older bardic poetry plus a concluding verse based on the accentual song metre. Among other outstanding achievements must be 'Úr-Chill an Chreagáin', easily considered one of the most outstanding *aislingí* or vision-poems in the history of the whole genre. A work of astounding lyrical sweetness, it will live on as long as Gaelic lives:

Ag Úr-Chill an Chreagáin chodail mé aréir faoi bhrón,
is le héirí na maidne tháinig ainnir fá mo dhéin le póig,
bhí gríosghrua ghartha aici agus loinnir ina céibh mar ór,
is gurbh é íocshláinte an domhain bheith ag amharc ar an ríoghain óg.

[Ó Buachalla]

An early printed version of the Irish text published by the scribe Nicholas Kearney in the *Transactions of the Ossianic Society* has an accompanying English translation:

Near the clay of the church of Creggan I slept last night in Sorrow,
And with the dawn of morning a maiden approached me with a kiss,
Her cheeks blushed like the rose and her hair glistened like gold.
Twas the pleasure of the world to be gazing at the young princess.

The fairy calls the poet to come away from the worries of this world,
and after much to-ing and fro-ing he finally denies the invitation and
declares that he wants to be buried where he is now, in the graveyard of
Creggan:

má éagaim fán tSeanainn, i gcrích Mhanainn, nó san Éiphte mhór,
gurb ag Gaeil chumhra an Chreagáin a leagfar mé i gcré faoi fhód.

Though I die by the Shannon, in the Isle of Man or in great Egypt
It is in sweet-scented clay of Creggan that I shall lie under the sod.

It is a comfort to know that Mac Cumhaigh's fervent and heartfelt
wish came true. In the beautifully kept graveyard beside the Church of
Ireland in Creggan is a gravestone, which shows where Art Mac
Cumhaigh is buried. Just beyond the low wall there is a river and a wide
bend in the river. When I was last there, the rustle of wind in the trees,
the play of water on the bend in the river and the general peacefulness
of the place added up to an understanding of how the gift of inspiration
for a poem like 'Úr-Chill an Chreagáin' could come. Interestingly, in the
grounds of the churchyard is the actual tomb of the Ó Néills of the
Fews, where many other Ó Néills are also buried. It was discovered
accidentally when the graveyard was being renovated, and an exca-
vating machine ploughed into a hole in the ground. It is intriguing to
think that Art Mac Cumhaigh might have been sheltering in the very
tomb, with the bones of the Ó Néills all about him when he wrote:

Is é mo ghéarghoin tinnis gur theastaigh uainn Gaeil Thír Eoghain,
agus oidhríbh an Fheadha, gan seaghais faoi léig 'ár gcomhair,
géagaibh glandaite Néill Fhrasaigh nachar dhiúlt do cheol,
chuirfeadh éide fá Nollaig ar na hollaimh bheadh ag géilleadh dóibh.

Tis my sore wounded plague that we have lost the Gaels of Tyrone
And that the heirs of the Fews sleep without pleasure under the
stone hard by
The comely shoots that sprang from Niall Frasach who would not
leave music without its reward,
Who would give raiment at Christmas to the Ollamhs who owned
their sway.

[Ó Buachalla]

For many of us, the finding of the tomb of the Ó Néills like this is
something akin to the opening of the tomb of Tutankhamun. It seems
to make perfect sense why a poem of such incomparable lyrical sweet-
ness and deep elegiac beauty could have been written in a place like
this. It reminds me of a story once told to me by the late Michael
Hartnett – that when the bodies of the Pharaohs were being moved
from their tombs by boat down the Nile, the *fellahin*, the local people,
followed for ages on both sides of the river, crying and wailing and
ululating in mourning for the bodies of their erstwhile kings.

The graveyard at Creggan is an example of the wonder and magic
that a little care and consideration of the importance of local literary
tradition can grant us. Poems can come from everywhere and nowhere,
out of the deep blue sea and out of the elusive sky. If I knew what made
a poem, I would bottle it and sell it. But one thing I know for sure –
poems create other poems. Stories and songs beget other stories. They
change form, language, genre, but the more they are retold, the more
they add to the sum total of human pleasure and happiness.

We must not forget the importance of literary activity *in situ*, and I
hope that the centuries of literary activity in Irish will be cherished as
an important dimension of our popular culture and not left purely to
the devices of the scholarly elite. Public access to that tradition, one
way or another, will not be denied.

*A transcript of a lecture given in Queen's University Belfast in
December 2001.*

Kismet
or The Workings of Destiny

When I left Holland on our 'final return' to Turkey in the autumn of 1974, I had no idea what was ahead of me. All I knew was that I was five months pregnant and, by a miracle of bad timing, out to see the world. We travelled first by train to Zurich to visit my husband's favourite sister, Aysel, who was bringing up two small children while her German husband Nick, an ornithologist, was finishing his PhD on the bird-breeding patterns of Mt Oerlikon, or whatever it was. On the night train from Utrecht I caught an early glimpse of the real world beyond my sheltered life as a *luftmensch*, or sky-cadet, from which I had been used to looking at things. When the night porter suggested that for twenty Dutch florins he would ensure we were not disturbed, I was not so dumb as not to understand what that meant – turn him down and he would see to it that every other passenger was dumped into our compartment at all hours of the night. He would also see to it that the customs and immigration officers in Switzerland gave us a thorough going-over in the depths of the night. I was genuinely horrified. This was an abject bribe, and I could hardly believe my ears to hear it coming from a smiling young Dutchman. Where was all that Lutheran probity? Where was the genial image of the friendly Dutch? They were nothing to the Dutch idol of worship, which was money. Needless to say, we gave him the bribe, and slept soundly until we reached our destination.

For the second time in my life I was taking part in an unseasonable contraflow migration, just like in the fifties when my family returned to Ireland as everyone else was going in the opposite direction. In

Zurich my sister-in-law gave us sound advice while we made final preparations to return to a country that most people at the time were fleeing, mostly for economic reasons. Most importantly, she gave us food for the journey – *yolluk*, consisting of a large batch of *boşnak* or *kol böreği* or potato pastries in the Bosnian style, which was a speciality of her mother's side of the family. This and two cooked chickens made up the bulk of a hefty amount of food that was to bring us safely to Turkey.

We were to travel on the Orient Express. At the time it had come down enormously from the high-class railway immortalised by Agatha Christie in *Murder on the Orient Express*, and was a mixum-gatherum of two different trains, one starting out from Paris and the other from Munich. They met in Belgrade and from there trundled on as best they could as far as Sirkeci Station in Istanbul – the modern, luxurious equivalent of the old train was not even a gleam in the eye of some clever travel operator. We took a train from Zurich, which travelled over the famous Simplon Pass and Tunnel. I only realised we were climbing the mountain in spiral fashion from the inside when I noticed, in one of the odd breaks into the outside, that I had seen the same landscape at least three times already – truly an extraordinary act of modern engineering.

We reached Milan and changed trains, and there I had another glimpse of what lay before me. Near where the trains for the east came in stood a man with a small kiosk selling the life-size, elaborately dressed dolls in large boxes ostentatiously displayed on many young marriage beds, which were particularly loved by Yugoslav workers travelling home. 'Watch him, and keep a good eye on the luggage,' Dogan said, as he went to get cigarettes and a train timetable for the rest of our journey. He was right. Your man did seem a shifty type. Dark, with a large moustache, he was nevertheless dressed in an impeccably cut mohair camel coat. Something did not ring right. What was such a well-dressed man doing selling gee-gaws on a station platform? Was he a pickpocket? Did he make off with unaccompanied luggage? Or maybe he was no more than a small entrepreneur, impressed by the pervasive Italian idea of the *bella figura*. I never found out.

The pleasant journey along the great plain of Lombardy was made somehow mysterious by the great, heavily pollarded trees that loomed out of the mist. Short stops in Venice and Trieste were not long enough to take in anything more than the Square of St Mark and the Bridge of Sighs. Then we travelled through a rolling, well-farmed landscape studded with new chalet-type houses all the way to Belgrade. The level of housing was impressive and so was the intensive farming. Not an inch was wasted. Knowing that these houses had been built mostly by remittances sent back by members of farm families working in the parts of Europe we had come from, mostly Holland, France and Germany, did nothing to lessen their pleasantness. Actually, coming from a family which a generation before had sent huge remittances (half my mother's pay as a GP in England) back home to educate her siblings and keep up the farm, made me particularly susceptible to enjoying the pleasant industriousness through which we passed. Once, very early in the morning, I saw a pheasant roosting on the lowest branch of a tree at the edge of a tidy beech forest. Years later during the Bosnian war, as Serb and Croat forces thrashed each other back and forth through the Krajina, news footage of the same areas showed unforgettable scenes of those beautiful chalets in still-smoking ruins and the good farmland between them desolate and either overgrown or shattered by craters.

During the journey we met a Turkish girl called Ayse who was bringing – I am loath to say smuggling – two heavy suitcases of designer clothes from Milan back to sell in a boutique in Istanbul. When we got to Belgrade she and my husband went to get a couchette, for the rest of the journey. They both knew the score, that if you didn't manage to get a bed you had to sit it out all the way to Istanbul. I was left with the enormous pile of luggage. The train shunted back and forward. There was an incessant cacophony of shouts in languages I couldn't understand. It seemed to go on forever. I stood out on the little balcony at the door of the end carriage hoping against hope that either of the two would turn up. No such luck. More shunting back and forward. The part of the train we were on seemed to have ended up on another platform altogether. I definitely began to panic. I also began to feel distinctly queasy.

As I was blocking the passage to the door with my enormous stomach, some men whom I took to be Turkish workers began to speak to me. At this stage I had got as far as chapter sixty-two (the related past-perfect conditional) of *Türkische Sprachlehre für Ausländer* from the School of Oriental Studies in Vienna – the only book that I have ever read that in its method does justice to the logicality of the Turkish language. It had been a hard slog, necessitating I learn as least as much German as Turkish, but it meant that I now had some knowledge of a subject that I have always loved and have prided myself as being quite good at – grammar. So I knew, in theory at least, all about gerunds and gerundiums and present and past particles and the myriad suffixes and affixes, prefixes and postfixes from which a Turkish sentence is constructed. In my sheer terror I heard myself blurting out a sentence of perfect aggluti-native construction – '*Kocam geleceğim diye, gitti gelmedî* ('my husband having said he would be back soon, went away and hasn't come back'), all of which is only five highly inflected and conjugated words in Turkish and which persuaded the listeners that I was an excellent speaker of that language. This sentence drew forth a torrent of speech, of which I understood only one word in ten. Little did anybody around me know at how much of a loss I was. It would take at least five years of living in Turkey before I could make a complicated sentence like that with anything resembling a similar insouciance. As they say in Irish – *múineann gá seift*. Necessity is the mother of invention.

Eventually my husband and Ayse turned up and we manoeuvred ourselves into the part of the train that had the couchettes. My queasiness having turned into an honest-to-God bout of vomiting, we settled in for the last part of the journey. Thank God for the *yolluk*, which saved our lives, as there was no restaurant car between Belgrade and Istanbul. We shared it with a young American student, who was travelling to Pakistan to study the sitar under Ravi Shankar. Or at least that is what he thought he was doing. A product of your average middle-class Western democracy, like me, he was actually clueless. If it hadn't been for Aysel's carefully packed hamper he would have died of inanition even before reaching Istanbul. Before leaving us he solemnly presented us with an American silver dollar in a little gift box as a thank you for having kept him from starving. His father had assured him that nothing else would be as welcome a gift in the countries he was travelling through. Even then, despite my innocence, I had a suspicion that a few paper dollars, actual everyday currency, would be a much more effective, more appreciated, and lighter stash of gifts. I don't remember whether we exchanged addresses or not. Anyway, we never heard from him again. I wonder if he ever did make it to Pakistan. Iran was particularly tricky at the time, it being shortly after the popular revolution had ousted the shah, and just before the mullahs hijacked the uprising of the mostly left-wing muhajaddin. I somehow doubted that Ravi Shankar would have accepted him as a pupil on the sitar, unless he had shown very particular musical talent. Maybe he was just a slightly belated hippy going on to Nepal and either making it home eventually or not. I never found out.

We on the other hand had enough on our plate. The train eventually limped into Sirkeci Station in Istanbul ten hours late. We had been held up by the Bulgars insisting on exorbitant transit visas, smiling and calling us 'komşu, komşu' ('neighbour'), while perpetuating highway robbery. Then there was the long wait at the Turkish border station of Kapıkırı. As we had slept mostly through Bulgaria it was morning when we travelled through the countryside of East Thrace or Trakya, the European province of Turkey. After the rolling farmlands and tidy chalets of Yugoslavia it seemed irredeemably run down – nothing but small, one-storey houses in villages that often seemed little more than an assortment of badly built shanties. The harvest of hay and maize was already gathered, and the fields looked poor and bare under the looming fog. Preparation of the fields for the planting of winter wheat had already begun, and the only movement in the whole countryside was that of the odd tractor making straight brown lines in the yellow stubble. Dogan and I stood side by side, not saying a word – he because he was deeply ashamed of the first appearance of his country, and I because I didn't want to make him feel ashamed. It was all very much a sorry sight.

An even sorrier sight awaited us in Sirkeci. The poor Turkish workers, coming by longer train journey rather than by coach because it was cheaper and easier to bring more stuff, were beset by and shouted and screamed at by the customs officials. Miserable cardboard boxes tied up with string were torn open and their contents strewn all over the place. Again, all this shouting in a language I could not understand. I wondered what the fuss was about. Later I discovered that being a customs official was a big deal, and entitled you to bribes both small and large for letting people bring into the country material, some of which was their constitutional right, most of which was not. The really big bribes – mostly for contraband – went to those stationed in Kapıkırı, and the officials in Istanbul were pretty pissed off at only having the poorest and most innocuous workers on whom to vent their anger. Turkey at this time had a high-tariff protectionist economy, for all the world like the Ireland of the fifties. One of my earliest childhood memories dates back to that decade and it is of being so tiny I had to take two steps for my father's every one step. All I could see was the holed pattern on my father's brown leather brogues as he held my hand and walked back and forth in a small lean-to near the customs post off the boat from Liverpool. Don't ask me what they were looking for being smuggled in from the austerity of post-war England. Nylon stockings and the likes, I suppose.

There is a great story of my grandfather taking my granny to Paris after the war. It was the first time he had been back there since his stint at the Sorbonne, where as a student at the Collège des Irlandais he had got an arts degree way back in the year dot, sometime at the turn of the century. My granny had a great friend, a Mrs McCurtain, to whom she had promised to bring back a hat from Paris. 'Do you have anything else to declare, Ma'am?' said the customs officer, unable to bring himself to look in the direction of her ample bosom. 'Not in the least, young man,' said my granny blithely, only afterwards realising that all the time an enormous pheasant feather had been sticking up out of that part of her anatomy, in the depths of which she had secreted the notorious hat.

But fraught and all as such minutes were, they were nothing to what I witnessed in Sirkeci. It was like a scene out of Hell. The poor unfortunate workers, mostly from Germany, were the targets of great jealousy and resentment by the petits fonctionnaires back home. If that was what Turks did to their own countrymen I dreaded to imagine what the scenes at the end of the long train journeys to, say, Auschwitz, must have been like. We, on the other hand, were whisked through on the strength of Dogan's student passport and my Irish one and my by now obvious condition. Our luggage wasn't as much as looked at. It was smiles for us all around. I felt terribly guilty. Relieved in part that we were not being subjected to such dreadful behaviour, but at the same time guilty for what seemed to be a totally unfair privilege. It all reminded me of being back in national school in Nenagh, County Tipperary, where kids around me were being beaten with well-worn sticks for not knowing Irish. I on the contrary was above reproach because I had better Irish than the teachers and spoke in *tuiseals*, automatically inflecting words, because that is what you do when you know an inflected language. Once again, I had got away with murder. Or that was how it seemed.

But that moment didn't last for long because shortly we were descended upon by the extended family – Dogan's mother, his two sisters and his youngest sister's husband Emin, who was the only car owner and designated to bring us all the way across the Bosphorus to where Dogan's mother lived in a small ground-floor flat of a two-storeyed house in Küçükyalı. They had come to collect us at five in the morning, when the train was supposed to have got in. After waiting a few hours, they had gone back home, had a few hours' sleep, and were back waiting for us again. They seemed to think nothing of the ten-hour *retar*, as goes the Turkish word, borrowed from the French. I was gradually learning that time in Turkey was different from time in northern Europe. More like Irish time in fact, these still being the days when to give a person a time to meet in Ireland meant at the very earliest twenty minutes later. I had always found this a problem because for my surgeon father, good timekeeping was of the essence: in an operating theatre, where people's lives are at stake, one is scrubbed up and ready for work at half past eight on the dot. It is just not up for discussion. Later I found out that Turks, when they want to be, are very good time-keepers. It is not for nothing that they are called the Prussians of the Levant. But that is something I discovered much later, in my professional life. Right now I was just *yenge*, the auntie that married in. And having no obvious or ostensible family structure or kin to back me up, I was an *el kızı*, literally 'hand maiden', which, in a society of complicated kin structures, was the lowest possible form of life within the family.

First there was the Bosphorus Bridge to be marvelled over. It had been opened just before in 1973 to celebrate the fiftieth year of the republic, and was an object of great national pride. Although we mostly used the ferryboats back and forth to the Old City from the Asian coast where most of the family lived, it was still a remarkable experience. Built perfectly on time by a British engineering firm, it was the first time the Bosphorus had been crossed by bridge since Roman times or even further back since Darius the Persian had built a pontoon to ferry his huge invading army across into Greece. My first footfall in Asia. I paid special attention to what seemed to me an important building, a rectangle of white marble, boarded up and abandoned just beside the deep cut the new road had made as the bridge abutted on the Asian shore. I later found out it was a military kiosk and given the ubiquitous ancientness of Istanbul's antiquities, quite unspectacular. But to me that day it was important. I still mark it off mentally every time I cross the bridge.

Later, visiting Dogan's brother in the old business centre of Bakırcılar Caddesi in Tahtakale, across from the wall of Istanbul University and just up from the Süleymaniye *camii* or mosque, it became the most natural thing in the world to travel from continent to continent. You bought your little disk for the turntable for a risible amount, checked to see you were on the right boat, crushed up to the open deck in the front if it was a fine day, or to one of the enclosed decks if it was cold, and waited until the boat was full, and off you went across to another continent. To take the ordinary, workaday ferries across the Bosphorus is still one of my heart's delights. Leaving the Old City in the evening with the sun setting behind the Aqueduct of Valens, the fire tower of Istanbul University on the horizon, the kiosks of Topkapi Palace at the edge of the sea, and the main mosques of the Muslim world straddling the city's seven hills, is to my mind the most beautiful man-made skyline in the world. San Francisco has a fine skyline and the evening view of Venice is also breathtaking, but I have never in my life seen a skyline like that of Istanbul's Old City at sunset, seen from a ferry chugging along and minding its own business as it deposits the city's tired workers over to the Asian suburbs.

The journey itself is never boring. First, there are the inevitable *çaycıs* offering hot ruby-red tea in little thin-waisted glasses. You can usually buy Turkish coffee or some kind of herb tea as well. You don't pay for it immediately, but just when the boat is approaching the shore and you think it will be too late (or you will get away with a free one, depending on your mentality), up springs the *çaycı* and asks for payment, more or less at your own discretion, or so it seems. On the other hand I have never come across a case of him being short-changed. The price is so tiny, and the self-respect of your average Turk so strong, that often I have seen people in a crowd charging backwards against the wave of people and running after the *çaycı*, insisting they pay for whatever it was they had drunk. Then there are the travelling salesmen who will offer you the chance to buy every kind of useful gadget from carpet cleaner to egg beater – all this accompanied by a demonstration of the article in question and a rapid-fire sales patter that is often worth listening to just for itself. No article is too small, no gadget too recondite, that it cannot be extolled to the skies as the best thing since the sliced pan. That it is in a highly demotic and at the same time formulaic Turkish adds to the charm of the sales pitch. It is now as much a part of a vanishing sonic dimension of Istanbul as the cries of the *eskici*, the rag-and-bone man much like that of the Lancashire of my childhood, or straight out of *Steptoe and Son*, right down to the scrawny horse and cart. Then there is the whistle of each quarter's *bekçi* or night-watchman, or the winter cry of the *bozacı* who in the depths of night sells a concoction of fermented millet much loved by all, which unfortunately I cordially detest.

But our first egress to the Asian continent was by car. We settled into Dogan's mother's one-bedroom flat in the mostly retirees' suburb of Kucukyalı. The exact address was Mağarı Çıkmazı, which I came to learn means 'the-one-way-street-leading-to-the-cave'. The cave in question was a Byzantine building with a courtyard, the stonework intercepted by lines of brick, typical of that type of architecture. Nobody had a clue what it might have been originally – a church, a sort of *caravan saray*, a monastery, or even a *han* of some kind, and I never managed to find out anything more about it except to notice that in spring the tumulus around it was covered with wild white anemones, *anemone nemorosa*, a sure sign that in the not-too-distant past the area had been woodland. Now it was a place where sheep were herded before their slaughter *en masse* at Kurban Bayramı, or the Feast of the Victim, held six weeks after the end of Ramadan, and one of the major dates in the Muslim calendar. It is held in memory of Abraham's attempt to honour God by sacrificing his only son, and the Muslim version of the story is remarkably like the Jewish and subsequently Christian version, the victim in question being poor old Isaac. This is a story for which I have always felt an innate distaste but have a positive detestation of since becoming a mother. That it is one of the major mythical images shared by the world's three monotheistic religions is a very disturbing idea: the unquestioned sacrificing of the son to the father, and that on what seems the pathological idea of being asked to do so directly by God. Mind you, Isaac does escape in each version of the story, but just by the skin of his teeth. To my mind it is a legend that does no justice to any of the three religions that believe in it.

On the other hand the actual killing of the sheep on the feast day, usually by each head of household or by a special ritual butcher who will come and do the dirty deed for a small financial recompense or even the gift of the sheepskin, never bothered me at all. I am a confirmed meat-eater and the respect with which each sheep's neck is cut over a small hole in the ground, and the way the earth is allowed to soak in the blood, is deeply sacramental in its ritual. It is done mercifully and swiftly to the accompaniment of a prayer and has always made me and other observers of the act aware of the basic fact that our lives are lived at the expense of the lives of other animals. It has always left me speechless for a long time afterwards and very aware of some of the conundrums and deepest realities of human existence. Later on I was to have a son who at the age of ten quite cold-bloodedly filmed the whole ritual on a video, including all the gory bits, while a daughter ran in horror into the bedroom, hid under the bed, and could not be coaxed out for over two hours. Another younger daughter, just barely able to speak, remarked quite nonchalantly '*Mey et oldu*', 'The sheepy-weepy has become meat' – proof of the fact that such things affect everybody quite differently.

Mağarı Çıkmazı was also the place where the sheep were penned for the lambs to be milked in the spring. You could buy the sheep milk to boil and use in making the most wonderfully creamy yoghurt imaginable. I was a strictly European eater of fruit yoghurts only until I became acquainted with sheep-milk yoghurt. It became an addiction. The only thing that was even better was a yoghurt from the town of Yalova made from water-buffalo milk. It had a large head of cream on it and was so thick you could cut it with a knife, and this was without the addition of clotting agents such as carrageen, which are now common-place, unfortunately even in Turkey. It became my *aş ermek*, or the food craving that pregnant women are allowed and even expected to develop in Turkey, where it is absolutely taboo to eat anything in the presence of a pregnant woman without offering her some. This is done in case she might develop a longing that she would be too polite to express. An unrequited longing for food in a pregnant mother is considered to be very harmful to the baby. It might mean the baby would be born with its tongue hanging out. Failing such an obvious symptom of foetal trauma, the baby might be born extremely greedy. Or impossible to satisfy. Or it might develop into a selfish and unsociable being, whose *gözü doymaz*, or 'eye', could never be replete – in effect, someone who is always and ever 'on the make', and never at peace with themselves or their surroundings.

There are a lot of people of this sort in Turkey, as there are now in Ireland and in every other country I have ever visited. Nevertheless, a certain peace of mind, or acceptance of one's fate, a type of active fatalism – to be able to learn what one can change and what one cannot change and to know the difference between them – seems to be deeply ingrained at the heart of civil Turkish society. So by allowing a pregnant woman to hanker even unconsciously after an item of food is a sure-fire way of creating a monster of the unborn child. Whether or not any of this has a whit of standing in scientific literature is totally beside the point. What it makes for is a great politeness and care generally shown to pregnant women in Turkey, which was exactly what was shown to me, and for which I remain eternally grateful.

But not every cultural difference was as easily reconnoitred. On the morning of the second day my mother-in-law put a large tray of string beans into my lap and said: '*Kız, temizle bunları.*' I understood I had to prepare them for cooking in some fashion or other but my only previous experience of any kind of bean having been those of Heinz in a tin I was at a complete loss. Dogan somehow explained to her that beans don't grow where I come from (a lie of course) and it got me off the hook. The late afternoon of the following day she had a *kris*, or some sort of nervous crisis. She shook and perspired and huffed and puffed until we brought her by taxi to the doctor. He was pretty cursory in his diagnosis and it was obvious that she had presented at his surgery in the past with almost the same symptoms. It was all very mysterious. Now, it was not for nothing that for years I had been bringing the laden tea tray into the drawing room to my mother while she had been doing a roaring trade in psychosomatic diseases. I was convinced this was a disease of the same nature, and took it as a personal attack against me as a daughter-in-law, an incompetent and heathen one at that. But I kept my thoughts to myself and held her hand through her ordeal. Just because a disease is hysterical or psychosomatic doesn't necessarily make it hurt any less. Dogan also had his suspicions and he also kept them to himself. He was convinced that this was an attack directed not so much at me as at him for being an ungrateful son and having taken his time getting an education in Europe while leaving his poor mother to struggle at home. And then to cap it all, here he is at home without a fortune to spend on her and a heathen wife in tow to boot.

Only years later did we compare notes and realise that we had both understood what was up, only had each blamed ourselves for it. After a few weeks of this, Dogan's younger brother Ufuk had her admitted to hospital, where she had an operation for what she called kidney stones. These were large enough stones that she passed regularly in her stool, washed and collected and brought to the doctor. The surgeon was mystified, because the operation showed she had no such complaint. Nor had she gallstones or any other stones that the body could possibly manufacture. Only later did we find out that before breakfast every morning she religiously drank a whole glass of olive oil, mixed with the juice of one lemon. The olive oil solidified in her bowel and created the mysterious stones. This was at least her third operation and she went on to endure two more, the last one being in Ireland and netting her a 'European scar' which she was not loath to display to all and sundry as if it were a triumphal trophy. Five major operations and all for nothing. Because my mother-in-law's ailment was not of a physiological nature – she was suffering from Münchausen's disease.

Münchausen's disease is named after the legendary German fabulist. The patient learns to mimic the symptoms of a particular illness so brilliantly that physicians and surgeons submit the patient to an operation, where no sign of any disease is ever discovered. It is a very difficult disease to diagnose and to cure, being at its core a masochistic need for the patient to undergo the trauma of surgery and also to benefit from the attention that being a suffering victim calls forth. An even more serious condition is Münchausen's by proxy, where the mother inflicts injuries on her child for the sake of the vicarious pity and attention she receives by being the mother of a suffering child – but this was something I learned about much later and had nothing to do with the problem at hand. I didn't know the exact diagnosis at this point but I had my suspicions. I distinctly remember feeling a bit miffed that she had only given us two days of relative peace before playing up. We had arrived on the Tuesday and she had had her first crisis on the Thursday.

Remziye Hanım, for that was her name, was in hospital for over three weeks and this period was like a honeymoon for us. We visited her every second day over on the European side of the city where her hospital, the Numune Hastane, was. The journey back and forth was great fun, and we also frequently visited Dogan's brother amongst the myriad historical monuments in the Old City. In Holland I had got hold of *Walking the Streets of Istanbul*, by John Freely and Hilary Somner-Boyd, and came to know a lot of the Old City through it. We bought a Redhouse Turkish dictionary at the famous Redhouse bookstore over in its old premises in Tahtakale. We bought Geoffrey Lewis's *Turkish Grammar*, still my *vade mecum* when I run into some Turkish construction I cannot quite fathom. On rainy days we took the tram from Sirkeci but mostly, when the rain stopped, we walked and walked. The streets after rain were lakes of water. I noticed the beautifully crafted stone gutters around the old imperial mosques and decided that Istanbul was definitely a city that had seen better days. In Ireland and Holland I had seen plenty of gutters but these were usually things that were being gradually improved over the years. Istanbul seemed to be the city that had invented gutters and then forgotten entirely about their existence. It was definitely like nowhere I had ever been before.

When Remziye Hanım got out of hospital, she was semi-invalid for a while. Then one day, when we had taken one of Dogan's nieces up the hills to look for *ciğdem*, or winter crocuses – basically any excuse for a long walk on a fine day – we came back early to find her down on her hands and knees, scrubbing the floors. She had not been impressed by my standards of cleanliness. She was indeed highly vituperative because in my attempts to cook in her absence I had damaged her exaltedly valued European Teflon non-stick frying pan. I admit I was only learning to cook à la Turca, but her reaction seemed totally over the top. To me it was only a pan, but to her it was both a status symbol and necessary for her minutely calculated diet, which was entirely low fat. There were bound to be difficulties between us.

I think, though, that one of the things that made her really angry with me was the fact that when we eventually went to Ankara, for Dogan to get work in MTA (Maden Tetkik Araştırma), the Geological Survey of Turkey, we went to visit his father, her estranged husband, and I got on particularly well with him. This was entirely a surprise to everyone, especially to me, who had been fed up to the gills with stories of his perfidy and iniquity. Even the fact that Remziye Hanım called him Koçero, the name of an especially notorious bandit in what was then called Kurdistan and is now for political reasons called the south-east of Turkey, had pre-judged me against him to the extent that when we went to visit him it was in some fear and trembling on my part. We arrived at the train station in Ankara towards night, and immediately the smog had us holding our breath. It was mostly caused by the low-grade coal or lignite used in house heating during the very cold winters of Ankara's continental climate. On the advice of one of Dogan's geological acquaintances in Istanbul we went at once to the Uzun Oteli at Dışkapı. The receptionist asked for our marriage certificate. And me in my condition! I was horrified, only to learn afterwards that there might have been a good reason for it, as the surrounding area had come down a lot in the world since Dogan's childhood and was full of tacky little hotels and night-clubs or *paviyon* of most dubious aspect. We went on foot to find where Dogan's father lived, in what Dogan remembered as a wooden house in a large garden full of all sorts of fruit trees, a duck pond at the front and a fountain playing in the courtyard. There was no sign of it. On every side of the large main thoroughfare that is Altındağ Caddesi there were itty-bitty shanties, shuttered and derelict. We pushed through a wooden door beside a *hurdacı*, or scrap metal collector, and there was a small glass lean-to with a large tree growing up through the middle of it. 'That is a mulberry tree, and I recognise it from my childhood,' said Dogan. We knocked at the door of the iron-roofed house beyond the glassed-in area. Dogan's stepmother opened it, and recognised him after a fourteen-year absence. We took off our shoes at the door and were ushered into a compact and clean little living room, in spite of the obvious poverty. Dogan's father, the infamous Koçero, came forward, we kissed his hand, and we were home.

The usual tea and pleasantries ensued. When we finally got up and insisted we spend the night in our hotel, there was pandemonium. Stay in a hotel? This would never do. It was unthinkable that a young man and his wife would not stay in his father's home. We prevailed and spent the night in the hotel, only for the pair of us to come down the next day with a whopping case of the flu. When Dogan's half-brother Cıhangır came by the next day to see why we hadn't turned up again, it was obvious that we would need looking after for at least a few days. So custom prevailed and, willy-nilly, we were moved bodily to Süleyman Leflef's house in the most insalubrious shantytown of Ankara, where we were plied with lemon drinks and aspirin and linden-blossom tea made from one of the last surviving trees in the once-glorious garden. We gradually got better. It seemed like a genuine case of *kismet* – destiny, or the hand of God, whichever way you prefer to look at it.

And so it happened that during the next five years, the person who had the greatest influence on me and who was my chief motivator in learning Turkish was my father-in-law, Süleyman Leflef. He was a great character, a genuine original. He had been the only male, and therefore literate person, left at home when the new surname law was promulgated in the twenties and when he went to register a name for the family under the law he just took the ending – *oğulları* 'sons of', off the long-standing family nickname, and so their surname became Leflef. When his older brothers came back from military service, they were very annoyed with him: 'Why didn't you take the chance to give us a heroic name like everyone else is doing?' A name like Safkan 'pure blood', or Öztürk 'original Turk', or Demirel 'iron hand', or the likes. He demurred, saying that the name they had had for hundreds of years was good enough for him and should be good enough for them as well.

A former military officer, my father-in-law had never really enjoyed his years in the army. For one thing, though a crack shot, he never believed in killing people. I remember years later when we finally caught a rat that had been terrifying the household, especially me with a newborn baby, he wouldn't even kill the rat. I, on the other hand, with more important things than rats' lives on my mind, drowned it unceremoniously in the nappy bucket. It was by default that he had ended up studying in Harbiye, the military academy. He had wanted to study at the Academy of Fine Arts, but did not have the necessary mathematics to be accepted. I once saw his graduation diploma, where he got top marks only in marksmanship and horsemanship. He had only advanced to the grade of *yüzbaşı*, or centurion, when he was cashiered for having two wives.

Being Muslim, Turks are allowed up to four wives by their religion. Since the reforms in Turkey brought about by Kemal Atatürk in the twenties, however, the secular, westernised state had outlawed polygamy. My father-in-law was given the choice of giving up the second illegal – but religiously accepted – wife, or being court-martialled. As a good Muslim he felt conscience-bound to keep the second wife, who had done him no wrong. And so, as he always maintained, he had resigned his commission because of his religious scruples. That was his version of the whole affair, but Remziye Hanım had a very different take on the story.

His philandering was the cause of her very genuine grievance. She was his only legal wife. She had, with her sister Mediha, been looking after the children of her Aunt Latife in Ankara when they had been followed by a young officer on Anafartalar Caddesi in Ulus, which was at that time the main street of the still tiny capital city. She was only fifteen years old at the time, and from pictures taken of her in Bosnian costume during her one year of schooling, was a remarkable beauty of the Balkan type. Süleyman Dede said he followed the girls because of their beautiful legs in short skirts, still a great novelty in the deeply Muslim but rapidly modernizing country. According to her sister, Remziye always said she wanted to marry an officer. Süleyman followed them home, noticed where they lived, one thing led to another and in a short time he presented himself in his full formal military uniform to ask for her hand, which he was duly granted. In their wedding photos they look a very handsome couple. Remziye's dress is of white satin with a train almost a mile long. She isn't wearing a veil, but a satin headdress, which exquisitely frames her dark blonde hair and her impeccable features.

But life with an officer did not have the glamour she had imagined. As his first commission Süleyman was sent to a village near Mardin, on the border with Syria. A fascinating area, it is still home to the Assyrian Christians or Süriyani, who use Aramaic, the language that Christ spoke, for their liturgical ceremonies. Such things held no interest for Remziye, who hated the climate, the lack of such basics as olives and who all her life went on about how the water was from underwater cisterns and had to be sieved with muslin to take out the little red worms wriggling in it. Having her mother-in-law come to live with them was no help either. Fatma, or Hamine as she was called by her complicated and extended family, was a formidable character and as tough as old boots. When, after some imagined slight or other, Remziye moved her own woollen mattress into another room, to sleep apart from her husband, his mother seemingly acquiesced to his taking a Kurdish servant girl as a sleeping partner. And a bald one at that, insisted Remziye, who always referred to her as *kel kızı*, or the bald girl.

There were other surprises and alarms to be endured. Once a visiting senior officer asked Süleyman to take a certain soldier out of the ranks and to beat him. Süleyman refused, as there was no reason to punish the soldier and he would be damned if he did so purely at a senior officer's say-so. The senior officer knew that Süleyman was correct according to military rules, but was still incensed. That night he sent a party of soldiers to arrest him and he gave the *vur emri*, or order that he should be shot at sight. Süleyman escaped with the help of the villagers and having appealed his case to a higher authority was pardoned and reinstated. But life with such a difficult, wilful and selfish man was very hard on Remziye. She missed the warmth, civility and modernity of her large Bosnian family. She detested her mother-in-law. She dearly regretted her marriage. And the birth of Dogan, her first child, while she was still sixteen, only a child herself, was not enough to ensure her happiness. The birth was very difficult. The child was two months premature, and she was in labour for three whole days with the dubious help of a village midwife and her cruel but extremely practical mother-in-law. In an area noted for its huge instance of infant mortality, especially from diarrhoea and dehydration in the baking Mesopotamian summers, it was through an enormous effort on her part that she managed to bring Dogan to the age of two. In a picture of the family and guests taken at his circumcision at the time it is hardly possible to recognise the sullen, withdrawn, painfully thin and worn young woman as the radiant young bride of three years before. Her dreadful unhappiness is utterly palpable.

Worse was to follow. On a subsequent tour of duty on the Black Sea, Süleyman took in another young woman called Lamiye. She was from a family of refugees from Selânik, and according to Remziye, a gypsy. When she arrived in the house, ostensibly as a servant, she had been so neglected that she had to be thoroughly washed and deloused. She regularly wet her bed. Then to top it all Süleyman went through a religious ceremony with her, a *hoca nikâhı*, that, to his mind at least, and actually according to Muslim law, if not the law of the land, made her his wife. She was to be his last wife, and if anything a *grande folie*. He was absolutely out of his mind about her. He played the *saz* and sang *uzun havas* (Turkish *sean nós*) like *Ezo Gelin* to her. He was prevailed upon, if only for the sake of his profession, to put her away time and time again, but each time he took her back. Remziye to her death declared that he had been given a love charm, that the girl's sister was a witch and knew how to bind a man irreducibly. Remziye, finally, throwing all hope of financial security and caution to the wind, complained to the military authorities. In the confrontation that followed Süleyman chose the young woman over a secure financial future and career in the military. He had been after all at Harbiye, the military academy, a classmate of Kenan Evren who led the putsch in 1980, and who made sure in the following years that the military would live high and well. To everyone who knew him the decision seemed like madness. To Remziye it was the result of evil machinations and a tryst with the devil.

So when she discovered that he had been kind to me, and that we actually got on quite well, she was understandably very seriously put out. Certain things happened between us and when, as a new mother with a six-week-old child, the tension between us had become so bad that my milk almost dried up, Aysel, who was visiting Turkey, realised that things could not go on like this and brought me to Ankara to stay in the shantytown with her father. There, for all the restrictions of shantytown life, the tensions were resolvable and my milk came back in by the bucketful. It was here, with the help of my father-in-law, that I can say I finally began to crack the linguistically hard nut that is the Turkish language.

Süleyman Dede was an Ottoman to the end. So much so that he refused to call Ataturk by that name. He was perfectly prepared to allow him the honorific appellation of *Gazi Paşa*, because he was just that – a great war hero (*gazi*) who survives, as opposed to a şeyit who dies a martyr's death. Ataturk was also a great *paşa*, or general. But to his dying day he refused to call him Ataturk, 'father of the Turks'. This he considered presumptuous in the extreme: 'How could anyone call himself "Father of the Turks" indeed! He is not my father.'

Not that he had any good words to say for his own father either, who had been an *ulema* or religious teacher in the local religious school, the *medrese*. He had also been a howling dervish, who with his fellow mystics would chant the holy phrase *Yaha Hu* for days on end until the whole building in which they sat began to shake. As a child, Süleyman had once looked through a keyhole at the ceremony and seen his own father in a trance state. He got such a shock that – though he remained an orthodox Sunni Muslim and even became a *hacı* as a result of making the pilgrimage to Mecca – he had no time for any of the dervish or mystic orders (the *tarıkatlar*). He looked askance at anything that could be considered radical, extremist or fundamentalist in any form. He also held it against his father that he had died young, leaving a widow to bring up a family of six sons on her own. His father had been blond-haired and blue-eyed, of that particular cerulean blue, which is not as rare as might be expected in Middle Anatolia. My father-in-law was usually scathing about light-coloured people, saying that they had no stamina and melted like candles in the summer heat. As well as his own father, he had in mind his wife, a Bosnian with the ash-blonde hair so typical of that part of the world, when he said this.

In spite of which he took to me enormously. Quite a demon in his youth, he had mellowed considerably by the time we met. He was in his own words *kurt kocaince*, 'an old wolf ', which refers to the proverb '*Kurt kocaince köpeklerin maskarası olurmuş*' ('When the wolf gets old and thin he becomes the laughing-stock of the dogs'). In some ways I was a kind of honorary man for him. He would call me out of the kitchen, saying '*Benim gelin mutfakta avratların icinde ne yapior?*' ('What is my daughter-in-law doing in the kitchen amongst the womenfolk?'), using in ironic manner the old-fashioned word *avrat* for woman, which might be better translated as 'female slave'. Likewise he didn't like to see me reading books, thinking it was a waste of time – time which would be much better spent in pleasant conversation with himself.

So we would spend hours talking to each other. When it was time for him to say his prayers, he went into the next room with his prayer rug, said them and then came in again and we continued the conversation where we had just left off. In the afternoons I would make him his *gelin kahvesi*, the special coffee made by the lily-white hands of the new bride, and he would drink it with great pleasure and we would continue speaking about everything under the sun. He never once suggested that I should convert, though once he set out to teach me the Arabic alphabet so that I could read the holy book *Koran-i-Kerim*. After three days of wrestling with *ayin*, *kayin* and I don't know what else, I proved to be a total *eejit*, and he decided that conversion was a grace obviously not vouchsafed me by Allah. I was fine as I was, one of the 'people of the book', *kitaplılardan*. As the *Incil*, or New Testament, and the *Tevrah*, or Torah, are considered holy books in Islam, the idea of conversion never rose again. After a few years I think I became in his eyes an honorary Muslim as well as an honorary man, and we got on together like the proverbial house on fire.

I remember one day one of his cronies named Berber Huseyn called by. I made *gelin kahvesi* in the usual small cups, and as they sat there sipping it I was an 'ear-guest' at their conversation, as the lovely Turkish expression for eavesdropping has it:

'She is very nice, for a heathen,' says Berber Huseyn.
'Indeed and she is, but you know those heathens aren't all bad people at all,' says Süleyman Dede.
'Oh, don't I know well. I have two sons in Germany amongst the heathens, and according to them, you couldn't find a straighter or more honest people on this earth.'
'If it weren't for the drink.'
'Yes, the alcoholic drink makes animals out of them. Animals entirely.'
'Yes, it is a real pity about the drink.'

This would have been amusing in itself even if it hadn't reminded me of similar conversations about Turkey I was to have in Irish with Thomas Murphy, my aunt's husband, and his cronies in a pub in the Gaeltacht:

'And you mean to tell me that the Muslims don't take drink at all?'
'No. They think that drinking is a mortal sin. It is against their religion.'
'God, that's hard. They must be a very straight people.'
'They are indeed.'
'And tell me one thing if you tell me no more: is it true that Muslims have more than one wife?'
'Yes, sometimes they can have more than one wife. Their religion allows them to have anything up to four.'
'Four wives. That's awful. They must make right animals of themselves to be even thinking of having four wives.'

Same difference. *Plus ça change.* This is the sort of thing that has always made me aware of the fact that so many things, whether ideas of dirt and pollution, or of inward and outward, edible and inedible, sacred and secular, are just lines that are drawn on the chaos of the world in a way that is highly culture-bound and pretty arbitrary, if not downright gratuitous. All cultures draw these lines; it's just that they draw them at slightly different places. Living à la Turca for five years at an early age made me something akin to an anthropologist. It was sharpened by feeling myself at home in a language so entirely different from Irish, and paradoxically, helped me focus more than ever on Irish. Being outside an English-speaking world for so long also made me aware of my other mother-language. This all came to me from learning Turkish.

The language that Süleyman Dede taught me was a Turkish that was colloquial, slightly old-fashioned and basically Middle Anatolian, rather than the more precious language spoken in Istanbul – just like Gaeltacht Irish, a language with a large stock of proverbs and formulaic phrases. Süleyman Dede's Turkish is located somewhere between the written and the spoken, perhaps with more emphasis on the spoken. This is best illustrated by its marked reliance on context. Who says what and to whom is very important, because of the construction of the language, where a single word may have an autonomous function to an extent unknown to us: for instance the well-known example, often used by me 'Irlandalılaştıramadıklarımızdanmısınız?' ('Are you one of those whom we have not been able to turn into an Irish person?') Unlike the sometimes amazingly long words in German, which are really chains of words, this is one single word with the function and meaning of a whole long sentence.

In spite of the huge differences in syntax, however, I recognised something in the language that made me feel very much at home. Like the Gaeltacht Irish I had learned as a small child, the appropriate use of a key word from a well-known story or from a proverb can either clinch an argument or cause general hilarity. All one has to mention are the words *ahu gözler* or *sırma saçlı olur*, 'almond eyes' or 'golden hair', and everybody knows you are referring to the apotropaic over-praising of the dead, from the proverb '*Kör ölür ahu gözler olur, Kel ölür, sırma saçlı olur'* ('When the blind man dies they say he had almond eyes; when the bald man dies they say he had golden hair'). This is a good example of a Turkish proverb in that it contains the highly characteristic parallelism and balanced structure of two complementary clauses. Also the two verbs *olur* 'to be' and *ölür* 'to die', have an alliterative and euphonic charm almost too strong to resist.

Then there is the whole range of colloquial language which stems from the stories associated with Nasreddin Hodja. According to the most reliable sources Nasreddin Hodja was born in 1208 in the Anatolian village of Hortu. He has become the delightful and inimitable personification of Turkish humour. He has also become a bit of an international celebrity, and his stories have been translated into many languages, including Russian and Chinese. His fame at home is assured, and, like the case of Homer, many towns in Anatolia vie for the exclusive honour of being his birthplace. The Hodja stories have been passed down chiefly by word of mouth and a wide knowledge of Nasreddin Hodja stories can be taken for granted among all Turks. He is the archetypal Turkish Everyman, and his down-to-earth humour and the sagacity of his repartee are redolent of the best of Turkish culture. His stories are so renowned that usually you only have to mention a key phrase from a story in the appropriate place in conversation to raise a laugh. By a process of metonymy, the audience supplies the rest of the story. And if someone doesn't get it, this is as good an opportunity as any to tell the story all over again from the start. '*Bir varmış, bir yokmuş, Bir gün Nasreddin Hodja ...*' ('Once upon a time, Nasreddin Hodja was walking along the road when ...').

Many stories about Nasreddin Hodja require some basic knowledge of Turkish life. One such story might very well be understood by an older generation of Irish people for whom *DV* or *Deo Volente*, 'By the Will of God', would be a phrase that was written in every letter and that tripped readily off the tongue. In this story Nasreddin Hodja looks up at the sky one evening and says to his wife:

'Tomorrow morning, if the weather is fine, I will go out and work in my vineyard. If it is not fine, I will stay in and work at home.' 'Oh

Nasreddin Hodja,' says his wife, 'you mustn't forget to say *inşallah* [by the will of God].' 'Woman,' he says, 'it has nothing to do with the will of God. Either the day will be fine or it won't be fine.'

Next morning, when he woke up, the day was fine so he hopped up on his donkey and set off for the vineyard. But on the way he was set upon by robbers. They stole from him and beat him and then loaded up his donkey and him and made them carry the loads all day long. Very late that night his wife heard a very feeble knock at the door. *'Kim o?* [Who is there?]' she asked. *'Benim,'* said a very weak voice, which she recognized as her husband's. *'Benim, inşallah* [It is I, by the will of God].' He had learned his lesson the hard way.

During my five years in Turkey, I came under many literary influences. According to Chinese sources, Turkish literature began in the second century BC, but the first extant records are those of the Orhon cuneiforms, generally dated to the eighth century AD. As the Turks moved westward, different branches of the language came into existence. The most important is Cağatay, which evolved its own literature quite separately from Ottoman. There is also Oğuz, the forerunner of modern Turkish. The most notable work produced was *Dede Korkut Kitabı* (*The Book of Dede Korkut*), which, like the early Irish sagas, has a prose narrative punctuated by superb poetry insets. Ottoman literature began in the early thirteenth century, with poets such as Yunus Emre and Esrefoğlu soon founding a mystic tradition of considerable value in Islamic culture. A riveting sample of this mystic tradition voiced seven centuries ago comes in the following stanza from Yunus Emre's poem entitled 'Aşkın Aldı Benden Beni' ('Your Love Has Wrested Me Away from Me'):

Aşkın aldı benden beni
Bana seni gerek seni
Ben yanarım dün ü günü
Bana seni gerek seni.

Your love has wrested me away from me
You're the one I need, you're the one I crave

Day and night I burn, gripped by agony,
You're the one I need, you're the one I crave.

This tradition of syllabic folk poetry, much of it marked by a mystic quality, was always sung to the poet's own accompaniment on the stringed instrument called the *bağlama* or *saz*. It continued as a live tradition down until the seventies and competitions for extempore composition of folk poetry are still held.

Persian forms began to exercise an influence on Ottoman poets, who gradually adopted and used them to create a new Turkish language now known as Osmanlı. Poetry inspired by Persian forms began in the mid-sixteenth century, reaching its peak perhaps in the work of Nedim, the most prominent and most Turkish poet of the Lâle Devri or Age of Tulips, which, like the subsequent period in Dutch history devoted to the same flower, was an age of excess and effeteness. Westernisation started in the late nineteenth century, and the work of Ahmed Haşim and his contemporaries combines Persian metre with themes prompted by the French symbolists. The emergence of modern Turkey produced poetry far more aware of its local, popular roots. Poets turned to take up the syllabic metres of folk poetry, and the old Osmanli literary style gave way to the more direct language characteristic of most western poetry.

In both Persian and Arabic, the literary language is poles apart from the colloquial language, but in Turkish, because of the extremely robust and widespread tradition of folk poetry, the language as it exists since the reforms of the twenties is not so polarised. The most famous folk poet of recent times is Aşık Veysel from Sivas province. Here is an extract from 'Kara Toprak' ('The Black Earth'), perhaps his most famous composition:

Dost dost diye nicesine sarıldım
Benim sadık yarim kara topraktır
Benhude dolandım yar, boşa yoruldum
Benim sadık yârım kara topraktır.

I embraced so many, thinking them a friend
My true love is the black earth
In vain I wandered, exhausted myself for naught
My true love is the black earth.

The kind of poetry composed by Aşık Veysel became possible not
only because of the depths of the folk tradition in Turkey, but also
because of the work of several major Turkish poets of the twentieth
century, especially Nâzım Hikmet, Oktay Rifat and Orhan Veli. Two
other main strains of poetry also affected me during my half-decade in
Turkey: the mystic tradition of Mevlâna Djellal a-Din Rumi and the
Osmanli tradition, written in Persian forms, mostly as *gazel* or *rubai*, as
the Turkish pronunciations of those forms go. Of particular interest to
me at the time were the poems of Mevlâna Djellal a-Din Rumi, so much
so that I used to go by bus to Konya every December on the treacherous
snowy roads, to watch the dancing dervishes of his religious order perform
the *sema* or 'dance' of the whirling dervishes. In one poem he writes:

Come, come whoever you are
Wonderer, worshipper, lover of leaving
It doesn't matter.
Ours is not a caravan of despair.
Come, even if you have broken your vow
a thousand times.
Come, yet again, come, come.

I took enormous pleasure in my exposure to Turkish literature.
Imagine my amazement and delight when a few years ago 'Toircheas I',
a three-stanza poem of mine, was translated into one short and three
long Turkish sentences, each sentence taking up nearly a whole stanza.
Similarly, another poem, 'Ceist na Teangan', was translated into two
very complicated sentences. These poems and fifteen or so others
were translated during a week-long seminar on one of the Princes'
Islands, Heybeli Adı, by a group led by the noted poet and translator

[59]

Cevat Çapan. After listening to the different possible suggestions, Cevat Çapan would keep his pen poised in mid-air until he was satisfied. Then, as I watched in amazement, he would come out with one perfectly enunciated, complicated, long agglutinative sentence of such elegant structure that it left me spellbound. I could appreciate enormously the verbal virtuosity involved but could never hope to match it myself.

Living an almost hermetically sealed Turkish lifestyle for five years was the greatest inducement I could possibly have had for writing in Irish. Outside the English-language *mentalité* I felt freed to deal with Irish on its own terms. Free of the conflict between my two mother-languages that I often feel when in an English-speaking environment. The five years I spent in Turkey contributed greatly to my ending up as a poet writing in Irish. Strangely enough, losing myself in the delights of my new environment, in the carpets and kilims, in the handicrafts of all kinds, in Turkish classical music and calligraphy, I came to appreciate my own language all the more acutely.

To this day I am enamoured of Turkey, the cradle of so many different civilisations and nations – Hittite, Urartian, Sumerian, Armenian, Lycian, Lydian, Bithnian, Gallatian – and among my favourites, the great cities of the Ionic Greeks. Not to mention later invaders such as Romans, Byzantines, Arabs, Turks of all shapes and forms, ending in the Great Imperial culture of the Ottomans and in the twentieth century, the founding of the Turkish Republic. The layer upon layer of peoples and cultures is astounding. I feel that if I am vouchsafed even a very long life I will never get to the end of it.

When I wrote the poem with which I will finish, I was informed by the best authorities that I was visiting the only known *Plutonium*, or temple of Pluto, known to have existed in the ancient world. Since then I have discovered that a few others have been uncovered, including one at ancient Nyssa, just up the road. Next summer I must go and visit it and maybe it will give me another poem. Of course, one of the main reasons for writing the poem at all was that I was so tickled by the two different meanings of 'Plutonium': the very old and the very new, all in the one word. Which to me goes to the very centre of the paradox that is Turkey.

Plútóiniam

    a tugtar air
iseatóp dainséarach radaighníomhach
is ar theampall Dia Ifrinn.

Tá's agam, bhíos ann.
I Hieropolis, an chathair bheannaithe,
láimh le Pamukkale na Tuirce,

tá an teampall, nó an poll
faoin dtalamh, an t-aon cheann
a mhaireann ón sean-am.
Níl cead isteach ann.

'Dikkat, girilmez.
Tehlikeli gaz var'
a fógraítear dúinn go dóite.

Ba leor san domhsa.
Thugas as na bonnaibh é
chomh maith is a bhí sé ionam

á rá gurb olc an áit
a thug mo chosa mé
is a chonách san orm!

Fós, in aimsir Strabo
bhí sagairt ann – na gallí –
imithe chomh mór san i dtaithí

na scamall nimhe go siúlaidís timpeall
beag beann ar a n-impleachtaí
is na daoine ag titim ina bpleistí
fuar marbh ar gach aon taobh dóibh.

Ba mhór an *power* é.
Ba mhór an chabhair é
chun greim docht daingean an uafáis
a dh'agairt ar an bpobal áitiúil.

É seo go léir dearmhadta
is imithe as mo cheann
gur chuala casaoid íogair
mo dhuine muinteartha
san ospidéal meabharghalair.

'Áit Phrotastúnach é seo.'
'Cá bhfios duit?' 'An tslí
a bheannaíonn siad duit
nó *ná* beannaíonn siad.'

Catshúil faichilleach thairsti aniar –
'Tá siad ag iarraidh mé a chasadh,
tá's agat. Teastaíonn uathu
go dtabharfainn diúltú dom' chreideamh.'

An bhean bhocht.
Do leath mo bhéal orm
is dhein dhá mhórúilí groí
dem' shúile.

Nó níl sé fíor
is ní raibh sé riamh
le linn a marthain féin
nó le linn saol dhá ghlúin
a chuaigh roimpi.

Ach b'fhíor dó tráth
le linn an Ghorta Mhóir
nuair a bhí an 'Irish Missionary Society'
go láidir i mbun gnímh
go háirithe i gCeann Trá.

Seo radachur núicléach na Staire
ní foláir. Fuíoll maraitheach
an drochshaoil is Ré na Súpanna.

Éiríonn sé aníos i gcónaí
is de shíor
ón duibheagán do-aitheanta
atá istigh ionainn.

Gal bréan an ocrais,
an deatach nimhe
ón bPlútóiniam, teampall
uafar Dia Ifrinn.

Plutonium

        is what they call
a dangerous radioactive isotope,
also the name of the temple of the Infernal Gods.

I know, I've been there.
In Hieropolis, the holy city
near Pamukkale in Turkey,

The temple, or the hole,
Is underground, the only one

Remaining from the ancient days.
Entry is forbidden

The grave warning read:
'*Dikket, girilmez. Tehlikeli gaz var.*'
'No admission. Dangerous gases are found here. By Order.'

That was enough for me.
I fled away as fast
As my feet could carry me,

Damning the place
And my curiosity
And my feet that brought me there.

Still in Strabo's day
The eunuch priests, the *Galli*,
Were so practised in breathing the poisonous clouds

That they could walk freely
Not caring for the deathly atmosphere
While people fell down in flocks
Dead on every side.

It was a terrible power –
It was the power of terror
That kept the grip of dread
Firmly on the local people.

And I had forgotten it all,
Cleared it from my memory,
Until I heard a mad line
From one of my family
In the Mental Hospital.

'This is a Protestant place, you know.'
'How would you know?' 'It's the way
They say hello to you,
Or say nothing.'

A catlike glance, alert, over her shoulder –
'They want me to change over,
You see. That's what they want,
Me to deny my faith.'

Poor woman –
My mouth fell open,
My eyes were wide
As millstones.

There's no truth in it
Nor has there ever been
In her lifetime
Nor in the two
Generations before hers.

But it was true once
During the Great Famine
When the Irish Missionary Society
Was manfully at work
And in Ventry above all.

It's the radioactive rain
Of History. A deadly residue
Of starvation and Soupers.

It rises up always
Out of the ground

From underworld caves
Within us:

A cloud of hunger
A poisoned smoke
From Plutonium, the dreadful
Church of the Infernal Gods.

Trans. Eiléan Ní Chuilleanáin

A transcript of a lecture given in Trinity College Dublin, on 26 February 2003.

An Chailleach agus an Spéirbhean agus an Saol Eile i gCoitinne

Ní fadó ó shin do scríobhas dán

Primavera

D'athraigh gach aon ní nuair a ghaibh sí féin thar bráid.
Bhainfeadh sí deora áthais as na clocha glasa, deirim leat.
Na héanlaithe beaga a bhí go dtí seo faoi smál,
d'osclaíodar a scornaigh is thosnaigh ag pípeáil
ar chuma feadóige stáin i láimh gheocaigh, amhail
is gur chuma leo sa diabhal an raibh nó nach raibh nóta acu.
Bláthanna fiaine a bhí chomh cúthail, chomh humhal
ag lorg bheith istigh go faichilleach ar chiumhaiseanna
na gceapach mbláth, táid anois go rábach, féach an falcaire fiain
ag baint radharc na súl díom go hobann lena réiltíní craorag.

Bhíos-sa, leis, ag caoi go ciúin ar ghéag,
i bhfolach faoi dhuilleog fige, éalaithe i mo dhú dara,
ag cur suas stailce, púic orm chun an tsaoil.
Thógfadh sé i bhfad níos mó ná meangadh gáire
ó aon spéirbhean chun mé a mhealladh as mo shliogán,
bhí an méid sin fógraithe thall is abhus agam roimh ré.
Ach do dhein sí é, le haon searradh amháin dá taobh,
le haon sméideadh meidhreach, caithiseach, thar a gualainn
do chorraigh sí na rútaí ionam, is d'fhág mé le míobhán
im cheann, gan cos ná láimh fúm, ach mé corrathónach, guagach.

Bhí sé de cheart agam 'Anois Teacht an Earraigh' a thabhairt air, ach ag an am céanna bhíos ag cuimhneamh ar dhá phictiúr de chuid Botticelli – *Primavera* agus *Breith Bhénus*. D'fhág san gur 'Primavera' a thugas mar theideal ar an dán sa deireadh.

Ach tharlódh sé leis gur 'Spéirbhean' nó 'Cailleach/ Spéirbhean' a bheinn tar éis a thabhairt ar an dán. Rud go mbeadh ciall leis, agus a thabharfadh siar isteach sa traidisiún Gaelach mé, idir an traidisiún liteartha agus traidisiún an bhéaloidis. Mar tá íomhá dhúbailte seo na Spéirmhná agus na Caillí chomh seanda in Éirinn leis an litríocht féin. Sa traidisiún liteartha ní gá ach an scéal ón tSean-Ghaeilge a lua ina luíonn Niall Naoi nGiallach leis an tseanchailleach atá i mbun an tobair. Deintear spéirbhean di ar an toirt. 'Mise an Flaitheas,' a deir sí agus deineann sí a thuar go mbeidh Niall agus sliocht a shleachta ina ríthe ar Éirinn.

Ní gá a lua anseo conas a chuaigh traidisiún na haislinge i gcion ar mhuintir na hÉireann thar na céadta bliain. Is leis a bhaineann cuid de na hiarrachtaí filíochta is áille agus is tarraingtí dá bhfuil againn – ó 'Gile na Gile' go 'Róisín Dubh', go 'Úr-Chill an Chreagáin', agus is boichte go mór a bheadh litríocht na Gaeilge ina n-éagmais. Fiú amháin litríocht an Bhéarla in Éirinn, cá mbeadh sé gan 'Oh My Dark Rosaleen' agus Kathleen Ni Houlihan: 'Did you see an old woman going down the road?' 'I didn't, but I saw a young girl and she had the walk of a queen,' gan trácht fiú ar shamplaí eile den rud céanna ar nós na brídeoige a léimeann ar mhuin an phríomhcharachtair sa dráma *Northern Star* de chuid Stewart Parker. Tharla go rabhas sa siopa gruaige áitiúil uair go raibh an dráma sin ar siúl i mBaile Átha Cliath. Bhíos ag cúléisteacht ar mo chomharsain a bhí ag biadán air seo is air siúd. Thosnaigh bean amháin ag caint ar an dráma a bhí feicthe aici an oíche roimh ré. 'And as soon as I saw that jilted bride I knew who she was,' a dúirt sí. 'She was Ireland.'

Ach is sa traidisiún béaloidis is mó a chuireas riamh mo shuim agus is ar bhéalaibh daoine a thángas trasna íomhá na Caillí ar dtúis. De réir dealraimh, bhí seanbhean thiar i nDún Chaoin darbh ainm Mór agus bhí mórán scéalta fúithi fós sa siúl agus mise ag fás suas. Bhí sí ag bruíon de shíor lena fear, Donncha Dí, agus lá amháin bhris ar an bhfoighne aige agus igh sé go mbeadh faid agus leithead Éireann idir é agus í. Deineadh san ar an bpointe boise agus ardaíodh tríd an aer é agus leandáladh síos é san áit gurb ainm Donncha Dí i gCo. an Dúin agus tá sé ann ó shin. Blianta fada ina dhiaidh san bhíos ag éisteacht le Breandán Feirtéar, ar Raidió na Gaeltachta, faid is a bhí sé ag cur agallaimh ar Hannah Daly, iarmháistreás poist Dhún Chaoin. Bhíodar ag caint ar scéal seo Mhóire agus ar cad a tharla dá fear. 'Agus,' arsa Hannah, nár chuir aon nath sa scéal, 'bhí daoine lasmuigh de thigh Challaghan sa Daingean tráthnóna Sathairn a chonaic ag gabháilt soir é agus paca ar a dhroim.' Amhail dá mba inné nó inniu a tharla sé. Chaitheas gáire. Ní thabharfadh aon ní aon sásamh dom go bhféadfainn dán a chumadh chun an líne sin a chur ann. Rud a dheineas, leis, tamall ina dhiaidh san:

Clabhsúr

… is ansan,
lá,
do bhailibh an dia leis.

D'éirigh ar maidin le fáinne an lae ghléigil,
rug ar a rásúr, a scuab fiacal is a *thravelling bag*
is thug dos na bonnaibh é.
Bhí daoine lasmuigh de thigh Challaghan sa Daingean
tráthnóna Sathairn a chonaic ag gabháilt soir é
agus paca ar a dhrom.

Chualasa leis, mar a bheadh i dtaibhreamh,
é ag gabháilt thar bráid,
a scol amhráin is a phort feadaíola aige
faoi mar a bheadh óbónna i dtaobh thíos den stáitse
'is é an dia Hercules, a ghráigh Anthony
atá á fhágaint' –

Anois táim folamh, is an poll seo i mo lár
Is n'fheadar cé líonfaidh é
nó cad leis? Dá mb'áil liom é a leanúint
ins an mbóithrín achrannach ...
ach ó, is fada fairsing í Éire
is tá iallach mo bhróg gan snaidhm.

Ar ndóigh, nuair a bhíos ag cuimhneamh ar scéal seo Mhóire, tháinig scéal eile a bhaineann léi chun mo chuimhne agus d'úsáideas an scéal sin chomh maith. De réir an scéil seo, tháinig uaigneas agus cumha ar Mhór i ndiaidh Dhonncha agus thug sí faoi thaisteal suas go híochtar na hÉireann ag triall air. D'fhág sí a tigh féin i nDún Chaoin agus nuair a tháinig sí go barr an Chlasaigh agus go bhfeaca sí paróiste leathan-aoibhinn Fhionntrá ag leathadh roimpi amach, do tháinig lagmhisneach uirthi. 'Ó, is fada fairsing í Éire,' ar sise, agus do chas sí ar a sáil abhaile di fhéin. Tá scéal eile a bhaineann leis an eachtra áirithe seo. Nuair a bhí sí ag casadh abhaile tháinig glaoch nádúrtha uirthi agus do dhein sí a mún taobh le bóthar an chlasaigh, agus bhí a mún chomh cumhachtach sin gur dhein sé an dá chlais mhóra ar dhá thaobh an bhóthair as a n-ainmnítear ó shin é. Thomas Murphy, fear m'aintín, bhíodh 'Leá bumbóire,' nó, 'leá múin Móire,' mar nath nó mallacht aige, leath mar mhagadh, agus ní bhíodh aon mheas aige ort mura rabhais ábalta ciall na bhfocal a dhéanamh amach dó, agus an scéal seo a insint.

Sampla is ea é seo de chomh láidir is chomh tábhachtach is a bhí íomhá na Caillí i meon na ndaoine agus i ndúchas an bhéaloidis. Tá seo fíor go speisialta i gcás na logainmneacha agus an dinnseanchais. Ba liosta le háireamh an méid baile fearann is móin is ard is tulach is loch a ainmnítear ón gCailleach nó a luaitear léi. Téann sé i bhfad siar roimh ré na gCeilteach, fiú. Mar a deir Gearóid Ó Crualaoich ina leabhar *The Book of the Cailleach*:

Old Europe was intensified in Ireland, where an abiding sense of a supreme, sovereign, female, cosmic agency appears to have operated on the incoming culture to a degree that resulted in a continuing, powerful sensibility to the presence in the landscape of such divine, female agency – a sensibility that has remained at the heart of Irish ancestral cosmology and mythological legend.

Tuigtear dom go raibh suim agam féin riamh is choíche san íomhá áirithe seo. Tá sé le tabhairt faoi ndeara sna chéad dánta a scríobhas go leomhfainn 'dánta' agus ní 'dréachtaí véarsaíochta a thabhairt orthu:

Teist Dhonncha Dí ar Mhór

Do sheas sí lomnocht
sa doircheacht.
a basa fuara – iasc gealúr –
ar mo ghualainn
a cromáin – tine ghealáin
faoi dhá ré a broinne.

Thumas mo cheann
i bhfeamnach a gruaige;
bhí tonn ghoirt na sáile
am' bualadh, am' shuathadh;
ár gcapaill bhána ag donnú
ina bhfranncaigh mhóra.
gach aon ní ina chorcra.

Nuair a dhúisíos ar maidin bhí tinneas cinn orm.
Thugas fé ndeara
go raibh gainní an liathbhuí ag clúdach a colainn.
Bhí fiacla lofa an duibheagáin
ag drannadh orm.
Sea, thógas mo chip is mo mheanaithe
is theicheas liom.

Nílim críochnaithe léi mar théama, fós, ach oiread, mar gach uair a thagaim trasna ar ruainne éigin den chailleach músclaíonn sí dánta ionam. Seo ceann cuíosach nua:

Eithne Uathach

An chéad bhean a luaitear
i mórshaothar Chéitinn
'Foras Feasa ar Éirin'
d'itheadh sí leanaí

óir 'do bhí ar daltachas
ag Déisibh Mumhan:
agus do hoileadh leo
ar fheoil naíon í',

chun gur luaithede
a bheadh sí in-nuachair
de bharr gur tairngríodh
go bhfaighidís talamh
ón bhfear a phósfadh sí.

Seans go bhfuil sí fós á dhéanamh.
Nó cad a déarfá
le Seán Savage, Máiréad Farrell
agus Dan McCann?

Cúpla bliain ó shin nuair a thug an scríbhneoir is foilsitheoir Micheál Ó Conghaile Léacht Uí Chadhain san ollscoil seo dúirt sé go raibh sé idir dhá chomhairle faoi. B'fhearr leis go mór, a dúirt sé, gearrscéal a scríobh nó tabhairt faoi cheann ar a laghad, fiú mura gcríochnófaí choíche é.

Táimse díreach ar an dálta céanna. Gach uair a shuínn síos le hiarracht a thabhairt faoin léacht seo a scríobh, is ea a thosnaínn ag scríobh dáin. Rud nach gearánta dhom ar shlí, mar is maith is eol dom nach ceart eiteachas a thabhairt don Bhé, pé uair a thagann sí id' threo. B'fhéidir go mbeifeá tamall maith eile ag lorg inspioráide is nach dtiocfadh sí. Ach mar sin féin tá léacht le tabhairt ...

Mar is léir ón méid atá scríte agam go dtí seo bhí suim mhór riamh agam sa bhéaloideas, cé ná féadfainn ag an am san ainm chomh hardnósach leis sin a thabhairt air. Ní raibh ann ach scéalta beaga a bhí fite fuaite mar dhlúth agus inneach tríd an gcaint agus mé i mo dheoraí beag cúig bliana d'aois thiar i dtigh m'aintín Máire i gCathair an Treantaigh i bparóiste Fhionntrá i lár na gcaogaidí.

Rudaí beaga a tharlaíodh ó lá go lá go luaití seanscéal leo nó tagairt éigin neamhghnáthach. Ar nós an lae, cúpla bliain ina dhiaidh sin, is mé i mo chailín óg, go rabhas ag siúl suas bóthar na Cathrach agus gúna síoda orm a bhí déanta de dhá stráice stuif a bhí fuaite le chéile agam agus fáithim curtha faoina mbun thíos – an t-aon iarracht fuála riamh a dheineas, agus an ceann deireanach. 'Ó', arsa John Sé, col ceathrair lem' Dhaid críonna, a bhuail liom ar an mbóthar, 'Is maith liom do ghúna.' 'Sea', arsa mise le teann mórtais, 'síoda is ea é.' 'Nach maith atá a fhios agam é', arsa John Sé, 'tháinig an méid sin síoda isteach san fhaill sin thiar ar a dtugann siad Faill an tSíoda, go raibh muintir an pharóiste ag ceangal na n-ainmhithe leis: "Bhí laincisí síoda faoi chaoire na Cathrach," mar a dúirt an file', – abairt a d'fhanfadh im' cheann go deo agus a léimfeadh amach chugam nuair a bheadh dán ar bun agam blianta fada ina dhiaidh sin.

Ní hamháin san ach bhí fear m'aintín, Tomás Ó Murchú nó Thomas Murphy mar ab fhearr aithne air, ar an tinteán agam. Fear é seo go raibh an-eolas ar stair an pharóiste aige, ní hamháin san ach ar sheanchas na seacht seanpharóistí laistiar den Daingean. Chuala oíche ina dhiaidh sin é i dtigh Dhónail Uí Chatháin, an tráth go raibh Oireachtas na nGael á thionól ag Breandán Mac Gearailt ar an mBuailtín. Bhí Máirtín Ó Cadhain sa chomhluadar. Tharla áiteamh idir Tomás agus Art Ó Beoláin maidir le suíomh agus tógaint sháipéal na Carraige.

'Tá sí tógtha ar an gCarraig,' arsa Art.

'Níl, ná an diabhal,' arsa Thomas, 'ach ar an mBóthar Buí.'

'Tá sí tógtha ar an gCarraig,' arsa Art arís.

'Cé dúirt leatsa é?' arsa Thomas.

'Nach bhfuil sé léite agam. Tá sé scríte sa leabhar.'

'Ó,' arsa Thomas, 'an té a bhreac an leabhar sin, do bhreac sé an diabhal d'éitheach!'

'Níl aon teora,' arsa Máirtín Ó Cadhain, 'níl aon teora leis an gcainteoir dúchais ceart.'

Timpeall an ama sin do thugas cóip den leabhar *Romantic Hidden Kerry* do Thomás. Cúpla lá ina dhiaidh sin do chuas á fhiosrú. 'Bhuel, a Thomáis, cad é do mheas ar an leabhar?' 'Níl sé olc,' a dúirt sé, 'téann sé siar dhá chéad bliain. Níl san olc ach raghainnse a ceathair duit.'

Ní áibhéal ar fad a bhí ann mar bhí a fhios aige gur piléar gunna mhóir ó árthach amuigh ar Bhá an Daingin a bhain an ceann de chaisleán na dTreantach a bhí ar an mbaile, in ionad é á leagadh ó bhád a bhí istigh i gcuan Fhionntrá, mar ba dhóchúla le duine. Ní raibh oiread is cloch os cionn cloiche den chaisleán sin ar an bhfód leis na céadta bliain. Seans maith gur in aimsir Dhún an Óir, nó ar a dhéanaí le linn chogadh na gCroiméalaíteach a cuireadh deireadh leis an gcúirt. Ní raibh éinne de chine na dTreantach ar leithinis Chorca Dhuibhne le fada, cé go bhfuil trí bhaile fearainn i bparóiste Fhionntrá ainmnithe uathu is go bhfuil an t-ainm coitianta go leor i gCiarraí thuaidh. Murab ionann is a gcomh-Normannaigh, na Feirtéirigh, na Rísigh, na Gearaltaigh agus muintir Hussey, ní raibh siad buan sa leithinis.

D'fhéadfadh Tomás dul siar seacht nglúin ina shinsear féin, bhí a n-ainmneacha go léir aige agus mórán eolais i dtaobh a saol. Deireadh sé gur rugadh a athair críonna féin ar an gCuan Uachtair, baile a tháinig saor ón mbleaist ar na prátaí i rith an Ghorta Mhóir. Ba bheag an mhaitheas dos na tionóntaí é, mar glanadh an baile agus dhá bhaile eile a bhí ar an gCuan, an Cuan Íochtair agus an Chúilín Bhán, sa bhliain 1867 ag athmháistir de chuid Lord Ventry, Corcaíoch darbh ainm Léithí. Deireadh Thomas i gcónaí go raibh a athair críonna dhá bhliain déag nuair a cuireadh amach as an gCuan iad. Chuaigh mórán de na tionóntaí go Meiriceá nó siar go Fán nó isteach ar an Oileán Tiar nó scaipeadh ar fuaid na dúthaí iad. Tháinig cuid acu ar an gCathair. 'Conas gur éirigh leo seilbh a fháil ar an áit anseo ar an gCathair?' arsa mise. 'Mar bhí an áit bán,' ar seisean, 'bhí nach éinne bailithe leo.'

Bhí a fhios aige conas a aistríodh an sáipéal i bparóiste Fhionntrá óna sheanionad thiar ar oirthear an pharóiste, mar a bhfuil an scoil anois ann, go láthair ar an Imleach Shlat a bhí tugtha saor in aisce ag Muintir Shé an Imligh. A uncail críonna Mícheál, a cailleadh go tragóideach díreach tar éis dó a dhul go Meiriceá, dob é an duine deireanach a cuireadh faoi ghuí an phobail sa seansáipéal, agus a aintín an chéad duine a baisteadh sa sáipéal nua. Bhí eolas aige ar mo mhuintir féinig, eolas nárbh fhearr leat a chloisint, uaireanta. 'Léan an phuis is na súile crothóige', a thugadh sé ar mo shin-seanmháthair, Léan Ní Chearna, lena rabhas in ainm is bheith dealraitheach. Nuair a bhíos ag cur suime breise sa Ghaolainn agus mé im' chailín óg is mó a thógas síos an seanchas seo go léir uaidh, ach is sia siar ná san go mór a théann mo chuimhní air siúd agus ar chuid eile de na seanphlandaí. Bhí aighneas agus gearrchaint a ndóthain acu, agus níorbh aon nath acu an teaspach a bhaint díot go tapaidh dá mbáil leo é. 'Leá bumbóire', nó 'Leá múin Móire ort,' an guí a bhíodh acu go minic, nó an mhallacht, ba chirte a rá agus bhí: 'Cá bhfios duitse, ní hamhlaidh go bhfuil Fios Fátha an Aoinscéil agat', mar nath leis acu.

Ach téann mo chuimhní orthu i bhfad níos sia siar ná san, go dtí an tréimhse a chaitheas thiar faróthu is mé i mo dhílleachta beag cúig bliana d'aois anall ó Shasana. Is cuimhin liom ag an tréimhse sin go raibh Johnny Long is a mhac Maidhc i mbun na feirme béal dorais is go raibh Jacksaí Sé is a dheirfiúir Neil sa tigh os a gcionn suas ar an mbaile. Bhí tigh John Sé i mbarr an bhaile is bhí de bhua ag an gcaidéal nó an *pump* a bhí acusan ina gclós nach dtriomaíodh sé riamh sa samhradh. Sheasaíodh gach fear díobh anairde ar mhullach a bhuaile féin agus bhíodh sé ag caitheamh gearrchainte is aighnis leis uaidh leis an bhfear eile. Ní cuimhin liom aon abairt dá ndúradar ach is cuimhin liom go maith chomh filiúil, dea-mheabhrach is a bhí an chaint acu. An aon ionadh más ea nuair a chuas i mbun mo chéad dánta gur ar an leibhéal seo teangan a thairgíos:

Mór Cráite

Tá Mór go dlúth fé ghlas
ina meabhairín bheag fhéin; 3" / 4" / 2"
ábhar liath is bán –

dearg (a bhíonn na créachta
a bhánn leath na gcuileanna
faid is a dheineann an leath eile a mbiaiste
ar fheoil na n-imeall).

'Éistíg', in ainm Dé,' ar sise leis na préacháin
is cabairí an Daingin a thagann san iarnóin
ag suathadh a mbolg.

'Tá na héinne dúnta isteach
ina ifreann féinín féin.'
Scaipeann na mionéin
nuair a chuireann sí scrabhadh scraith
lastuas díobh.

Bhí daoine eile ar an mbaile ag an am go raibh bua iontach teangan acu. I dteannta a bheith ina gcainteoirí dúchais bhíodar ina gcainteoirí maithe. An fear ba Ghaelaí ar fad acu, Tomás Mháiréad (Ó Sé), bhí sé caillte ón mbliain 1956, bliain díreach sara thángas-sa ar an gCathair. Ba é an duine deireanach ar aonteanga a bhí sa pharóiste é. Bhí sé de theist air nach raibh aon Bhéarla aige. Ní dóigh liom gur chreideas an scéal sin riamh ar fad ar fad. 'Conas nach raibh aon Bhéarla aige agus é ina chónaí ar an mbaile seo, áit a raibh "coastguards" le breis is céad bliain?' 'Nó ní thaithíodh sé iad. Ní théadh sé ina measc.' B'fhéidir go raibh smut maith don pholaitíocht i gceist chomh maith. Bhí sé orthu siúd a bhí ag an gcéad chruinniú poiblí den Land League i rith Chogadh na Talún, cruinniú a tionóladh i naomhóga i lár an chuain (200 éigin acu) nuair nach dtabharfadh Lord Ventry cead é a thionóladh ar an talamh. 'Na Parnells' a tugtaí ar a mhuintir le fada an lá. Ach mura raibh sé siúd ann, bhí mórán eile acu ann, Fitzie is John Sé is Jacksaí is a dheirfiúr Neil, is Joeín, is Annie Sheehy is a deartháir Jackie, is Johnny Long is a mhac Maidhc Long na Cathrach. Bhíodar ann go rábach, is má deirim arís é, go dea-chainteach.

Ach tharla rudaí eile i mo shaol agus bhailíos liom as an tír chomh luath in Éirinn agus a bhíos ábalta air. Tar éis seacht mbliana a chaitheamh thar lear, go háirithe san Ísiltír agus sa Tuirc, tuigeadh dom gurb é an rud is mó a theastaigh uaim sa saol ná filleadh ar Éirinn agus luí go lánaimsireach leis an scríbhneoireacht, dá bhféadfainn in aon chor é. Chuireas isteach ar bhursaireacht ón gComhairle Ealaíon agus fuaireas í, rud a thug mé féin agus mo bheirt clainne abhaile liom agus chuireas fúm i dtigh samhraidh mo mhuintire i gCathair an Treantaigh. Na 'Turcaís Bhána' a thugtaí ar na leanaí mar bhíodar chomh fionn san. 'Niúla agus na Turcaís Bhána' a bhí mar nath sa siúl ag an am. Bhíos ag gabháil do mhórán rudaí ag an am, úrscéal a chuaigh sa bhfraoch orm, cnuasach gearrscéalta a chríochnaíos ach nár foilsíodh riamh, ach thar aon ní eile do luíos leis an bhfilíocht. Ní raibh m'fhear céile fillte orainn fós agus bhíos an-uaigneach ansan sa tigh i m'aonar, agus na leanaí ina gcodladh, mé ag féachaint amach ar thráigh Fhionntrá agus an taoide tráite. Má bhí féin is i dtéarmaí an bhéaloideasa a chuireas mé féin in iúl, ag tarrac chugam 'persona' na Maighdine Mara:

An Mhaighdean Mhara

Má tá eireaball éisc féin orm
nílim gan dathúlacht éigin.
Tá mo ghruaig fada is buí
is tá loinnir ó m'ghainní
ná chífeá riamh ag mná míntíre.
Dath na gcloch atá sna súile acu

ach féach go cúramach isteach
i m'mhogaillse
is chífir an burdán fearna
is róinte groí
ag macnas
i m'mhac imreasán.

Ní gan pian
a thángas aníos
ar thalamh.
Do bhriseas
an slabhra réamhordaithe,
do mhalartaíos snámh
ar luail cosa,
ag priocadh liom
ar nós na gcuirliún.
Creid uaim gur grá, ní Dia,
a dhein é a ordú.

D'imís
is thógais leat mo chaipín draíochta.
Níl sé chomh fuirist orm teacht air
is a bhí sa scéal
i measc cearachail an díona.
Tá's agam
dheineas tochailt síos go dtí an gaíon
is níl aon rian de.
Theip an taoide orainn chomh maith
is tá francach ag cogaint na gréine

Timpeall an ama chéanna is ea do chuir Seán Ó Tuama in aithne do
Joe Daly agus don Bhab Feirtéar mé. Théinn ar a dtuairisc go minic
agus bhíodar an-mhaith ar fad dom. An-chuideachta ar fad ab ea iad,
an Bhab ina tigh féin, tine ghreadhnach síos agus cupaí tae ar siúl agus

Joe lena bhean Peig ina dtigh féin nó i dtigh Dhónail Uí Chatháin ar an mBuailtín. Is cuimhin liom ag an am gur thógas roinnt téipeanna den Bhab ag insint scéalta agus go seinnfinn dom féin iad sa leaba go dtí go dtitfeadh mo chodladh orm. Ní haon áibhéil a rá gur thángas go mór faoina n-anáil. Ní hamháin gur thug siad teidil agus scéalta frámacha mo chéad dá leabhar filíochta dom ach do mhúineadar dom chomh maith conas mé féin a chur in iúil trí chúinsí mo bheatha féin a athrú agus an t-amhábhar mothála a chlaochló, chun go ndéanfaí de rud níos uilí ná tarlachain bheaga phearsanta mo shaoil féin, nó rudaí róphearsanta, a bhainfeadh lem' shaol féin amháin. Do chabhraigh na scéalta liom an fhírinne a insint ach sceabha a chur fúithi, faoi mar a mhol Emily Dickinson tráth: 'Tell all the truth, but tell it slant', agus rudaí a rá ná beadh ar mo chumas a rá amach díreach.

Sampla den chur chuige seo is ea an dán, 'Féar Suaithinseach', teidealdán mo tharna cnuasaigh. An chéad uair a dheineas é a thaifeadadh, thug an Bhab leagan dom ar bhunaíos an dán air. Ní fada a bhí an téip déanta, áfach, nuair a scrios mo dheirfiúr é trí phopcheol a thaifeadadh anuas air, mar dhea is gur téip fholamh ab ea é mar nach raibh air ach caint!

Chuas thar n-ais go dtí an mBab agus fuaireas leagan agus leagan eile ach bhíodar go léir imithe ón leagan ar a raibh an dán bunaithe. Mar a tharlaíonn sé níor inis sí riamh arís mar is céad-chuimhin liomsa é; a rá go mbeireadh an sagart 'go haiclí' ar an gcomaoin naofa. Theastaigh an nath áirithe san uaim thar aon insint eile. An leagan a d'úsáideas sa deireadh ná leagan a fuaireas ón Ollamh Bo Almqvist, leagan a bhí tógtha ar téip agus ansan athscríte ag an Dochtúir Ríonach uí Ógáin.

Faoin am gur tharla sé seo bhí athruithe móra eile tarlaithe i mo shaol. Bhíomar tar éis trí bliana a chaitheamh i gCorca Dhuibhne. Bhí bliain acusan go raibh m'fhear céile ag obair i mBaile Átha Cliath, ag filleadh ar Chorca Dhuibhne gach re deireadh seachtaine. Thuigeamar go raibh an turas róchruaidh air agus go gcaithfimis bogadh linn go Baile Átha Cliath. Ba stracadh uafásach dom é an áit thiar a fhágaint agus ar feadh i bhfad bhíos an-uaigneach i ndiaidh na Gaeltachta. Bhíodh Raidió na Gaeltachta ar siúl agam de shíor, ar ndóigh, agus ar feadh roinnt blianta ina dhiaidh sin do dheininn smut de chlár le Maidhc Sé ar an stair áitiúil, go háirithe ón méid a bhíodh á léamh agam sa Roinn le Béaloideas. Ach is é Joe Daly a threoraigh mo chosa i dtreo na Roinne an chéad lá. Dúirt sé liom dul isteach ann, go ndéanfadh sé maitheas dom, agus ar seisean liom, 'Féach a bhfeicfir'.

Ar dtúis chuas ar thuairisc mo mhuintire féin. Thosnaíos ar ndóigh le Thomas Murphy. Más ea, bhí sé ann. Bhí trí scéal bailithe uaidh. Scéal mar gheall ar an iontas ba mhó, scéal ar an mbuachaill agus na pictiúirí beannaithe agus tosach scéil áirithe, 'An Luch is an Dreoilín'. Bhí Joe tar éis a rá liom go mbeadh an scéal san ann. Scéal is ea é atá sa *Seanchaí Muimhneach*, agus a bhailigh Pádraig Ó Siochfradha, nó 'An Seabhac' mar ab fhearr aithne air, i dtús an chéid. Faoin am a raibh Joe ag bailiú sna tríochaidí is sna daichidí ní raibh sé fanta níos mó i gcuimhne nó i mbéal na ndaoine. Bhí cuid den scéal fachta aige thall is abhus ach ní raibh tús an scéil ag éinne. Tháinig sé ó dheas go Cathair an Treantaigh d'aon ghnó chun tús an scéil a bhailiú mar go raibh sé cloiste aige go mb'fhéidir go raibh sé ann. Bhí sé ag Thomas. De réir an chur síos atá i dtús an scéil, is óna mháthair a chuala sé an scéal, fiche éigin bliain roimhe sin. Is é an cur síos atá air féin ná gur mac feirmeora é agus go raibh sé a hocht mbliana fichead d'aois. Bhí san fíor mar ní raibh an talamh fachta fós aige óna athair.

Ach is é an t-athair céanna Peats Ó Murchú an tseoid is mó gur thángas air. Bhí mórán cloiste agam riamh faoi Pheats, mar duine an-dheisbhéalach ab ea é agus bhí abairtíní dá chuid fós á n-aithris ag daoine le mo linnse. Mar shampla, rugadh a mhac Tomás, oíche sneachtaigh sa tslí go dtugaidís ina dhiaidh sin 'Tomáisín an tSneachta' air. Lá arna mháireach go moch ar maidin d'imigh Peats de shiúl cos thar Mhám na Gaoithe suas is bóthar na Leataithe i leith, ar a shlí ó thuaidh go dtí Cathair Deargáin, arbh as dá bhean, Cáit Foley. Lá sneachtaigh ab ea é, Lá Nollaig Bheag, agus bhí mo Neain ina gearrchaile beag i Leataoibh Meánach ag crústadh liathróidí sneachta ar a cairde. Buaileadh bleid air. 'Aon scéal nua, a Pheats?' 'Tá,' arsa é sin, 'mac ó aréir agam, ábhar fathaigh. Cnámha capaill óig faoi, is ní bhfaighidh sé aon fhuacht go brách.'

B'fhíor dó sa tarna cuid den chaint mar bhí a shláinte go maith ag Thomas riamh agus do ghaibh sé gan aon mháchail trí Fhliú Mór na bliana 1918, nuair a tógadh trí cinn de chónraí – dhá uncail agus deartháir leis – amach as an tigh in aon choicíos amháin. Ní raibh an fháidhiúlacht chéanna ag roinnt leis an gcéad chuid den abairt, áfach, mar cé go raibh sé tapaidh, aiclí go dtína sheanaois, ba fhada é ó thoirt fathaigh, sa tslí is go raibh meas mór aige i gcónaí ar an scrothaíocht. 'Níl aon teora leis,' a deireadh sé. Is beag a shíl sí, a deireadh mo Neain i gcónaí ina dhiaidh sin, go bhfásfadh sí féin suas, go mbeadh leanbh iníne aici, is go bpósfadh an iníon sin leanbh na hóiche sin aréir.

Ráiteachas eile leis a bhí fanta i gcuimhne na ndaoine ná an straidhn a bhí air le fear éigin a chuaigh ag áiteamh leis ag aonach an Daingin. 'Ar sin d'éirí in airde,' ar seisean, 'ar fhear atá i dtaoibh le dhá seanraga, seachas fear go bhfuil féar hocht mbó aige, i gCathair,' ag tagairt dó féin agus an-amhras aige as féin.

Ach ní go dtí go bhfaca mé an stuif ar fad a bhí bailithe ag Joe Daly uaidh a thuigeas cad é chomh maith de sheanchaí a bhí i bPeaid. Bhí na scéalta fada Fiannaíochta aige, scéal ar Bhalar Bhéimneach, scéal ar Fhionn is Rí Athadonáis. Ní hamháin sin ach bhí na cóirithe catha aige. Cóiriú catha an ghaiscígh, cóiriú catha an árthaigh, cóiriú catha na farraige. Ar feadh tamaill ansan do thógas na cóirithe catha sa cheann:

'Cioca ab fhearr leat,' arsan fathach, 'iomrascáil chruaidh chealgánta nó gabháilt de chlaimhte géara glasa i mbun is i mbarr easnaíocha a chéile?' 'Is fearr liom iomrascáil chruaidh chealgánta mar is í a thaithíos ar na faichibh fairis na leanaí uaisle.' 'Seo ar a chéile iad, bhuaileadar lámh in uachtar is lámh in íochtar is lámh i mbuaic na hiomrascála ar a chéile is an té a thiocfadh ó íochtar an domhain go huachtar an domhain ag féachaint ar dhá iomrascálaí is orthu araon ba chóir teacht ag féachaint. Do dheinidís talamh bog don dtalamh cruaidh agus talamh cruaidh don dtalamh bog, ísleáin dos na hardáin is ardáin dos na hísleáin. Thairgídís toibreacha fíoruisce tré chroí na gcloch nglas is trín screabhlach cruaidh aníos is na fóidíní gabhaidh a imíodh óna gcosa, bhainidís trí fhiacla as an gcailleach a bhíodh ina suí i gcathair Londan ag deargadh a pípe, agus ní stadadh na trí fhiacla sin trí bhogaithe is trí sléibhte go leagaidís trí chúirt a bheadh sa Domhain Toir. (Ó bhéalaithris Phádraig Uí Mhurchú, RBÉ 475: 602–3)

Thógas é seo go léir sa cheann. Ghaibh sórt éigin buile mé. Ghaibheas ó sheanchaí go seanchaí ag féachaint ar na leaganacha difriúla den chóiriú catha. Is ag Peats a' tSaoir ac' Loinsigh ó Bhaile an tSléibhe is fearr a bhí na cóirithe catha. Bhí sé tar éis scéalta a thabhairt don bhailitheoir Meiriceánach, Jeremiah Curtin, agus é ina fhear óg, thíos in Ard an Bhóthair. I nGaeilge is ea a thug sé na scéalta uaidh agus is amhlaidh a chuir a athair Béarla orthu do Churtin. Ach ní raibh Peats féin aon phioc sásta leis an leagan Béarla a cuireadh orthu. Nuair a bhí sé á dtabhairt amach san Edifón don bhailitheoir Seán Ó Dubhda ina dhiaidh sin dúirt sé:

Bhíos ag insint scéalta do Churtin agus a bhean a bhí ag scríobh agus bhí m'athair ag cur Béarla ar an nGaolainn di. Agus cheannaigh buachaill, mac feirmeora, do cheannaigh sé ceann des na leabhra sin agus bhí mo scéalta-sa thíos ann agus ní shamhlófá, ní raibh sé á chur síos in aon tslí ceart ná cóir ann mar bhíodar. Ní raibh an cóiriú catha in aon chor ann. Ní fhéadfaidís an cóiriú catha a scríobh chuige! (Ó bhéalaithris Pheats a' tSaoir 'ac Loinsigh, RBÉ)

An aon iontas ina dhiaidh san má bhí na dánta a bhí á scríobh agam ag an am lán den chóiriú catha de shaghsanna difriúla? Is é a tháinig chun m'aigne is leanbh ar deol agam, is mé ag iarraidh cur síos a dhéanamh ar an sórt domhain inar mhair an leanbh nuabheirthe ag an am, domhan lán de radharcanna agus de fhuaimeanna nach raibh sí fós ábalta ar a idirdhealú óna chéile, domhan úd na fuaime réamhshiombalaí, nó an *chora* mar a thugann an teoiricí feimineach ón bhFrainc, Julia Kristeva, air:

Ag Cothú Linbh

An eol duit an lá ón oíche,
go bhfuil mochthráigh mhór
ag fógairt rabharta,
go bhfuil na báid
go doimhin sa bhfarraige
mar a bhfuil éisc is rónta
is míolta móra
ag teacht ar bhois is ar bhais
is ar sheacht maidí rámha orthu,

go bhfuil do bháidín ag snámh
óró sa chuan
leis na lupadáin lapadáin
muranáin maranáin,
í go slim sleamhain
ó thóin go ceann
ag cur grean na farraige
in uachtar
is cúr na farraige
in íochtar?

Bhí dánta eile lán de na cóirithe catha chomh maith, dánta ar nós 'An
Rás'. Is éard a tharla anseo ná gur theastaigh uaim cur síos a dhéanamh
ar fhlosc agus faobhar ruaill buile nó babhta fiain tiomána suas faoin
dtír. Cóiriú catha an ghaiscígh a thairgíos chugam féin chun é seo a
chur in iúil.

Faoi mar a bheadh leon cuthaigh, nó tarbh fásaigh
nó ceann de mhuca allta na Fiannaíochta,
nó an gaiscíoch ag léimt faoi dhéin an fhathaigh

faoina chírín singilíneach síoda,
tiomáinim an chairt ar dalladh
trí bhailte beaga lár na hÉireann.
Beirim ar an ghaoth romham
is ní bheireann an ghaoth atá i mo dhiaidh orm.

Mar a bheadh saighead as bogha, piléar as gunna
nó seabhac rua trí scata mionéan lá Márta
scaipim na mílte slí taobh thiar dom.
Tá uimhreacha ar na fógraí bóthair
is ní thuigim an mílte iad nó kiloméadair.
Aonach, Ros Cré, Móinteach Mílic,
n'fheadar ar ghaibheas nó nár ghaibheas tríothu.
níl iontu faoin am seo ach teorainní luais
is moill ar an mbóthar go dtí tú.

Trí ghleannta sléibhte móinte bogaithe
scinnim ar séirse ón iarthar,
d'aon seáp amháin reatha i do threo
d'aon fháscadh ruthaig i do chuibhreann.
Deinim ardáin des na hísleáin, ísleáin de na hardáin
talamh bog de thalamh cruaidh is talamh cruaidh de thalamh bog, –
imíonn gnéithe uile seo na léarscáile as mo chuimhne,
ní fhanann ann ach gíoscán coscán is drithle soilse.

Timpeall an ama chéanna thángas ar leabhar *Italian Folktales*,
roghnaithe agus athinste ag Italo Calvino. Seo aistriúchán Béarla ar
chnuasach síscéalta a bhí aistrithe go hIodáilis ar dtúis ag Italo Calvino
ó theangacha éagsúla na hIodáile. Thógas an-cheann don mhéid a bhí
le rá aige sa réamhrá i dtaobh cad a tharla dó féin nuair a chuaigh sé
greamaithe i ndomhan seo na síscéal:

Domhsa ba léim caorach san aigéan é. Aigéan ina raibh mórán
daoine romhamsa cheana tar éis a thumadh, thar 150 éigin bliain,

ní lé dúil i nuaíocht nó sa rud neamhghnáthach ann féin, ach le creideamh doimhin go raibh eilimint dhúrúnda éigin ina luí ar an ngrinneall, eilimint nár mhór a tharrtháil ar son na teangan. (aistrithe ón mBéarla ag Nuala Ní Dhomhnaill)

Ón méid a scrígh sé tuigeadh dom nár ghalar éinne amháin an galar a bhí orm féin.

Do léimeas isteach sa domhan fó-thoinn seo gan oiread na fríde de dhúthracht intleachtúil ar son aon ní spontánaigh nó fréamhaithe nó bunaidh. Ba údar mór míshuaimhnis agam é bheith tumtha in eilimint éagruthach, eilimint a bhí chomh mall malltriallach san leis an oideas béil, eilimint nach bhféadfaí smacht coinsiasach a imirt air. (aistrithe ón mBéarla ag Nuala Ní Dhomhnaill)

Bhíos féin faoin am seo imithe ó na cóirithe catha agus na scéalta Fiannaíochta go dtí na síscéalta agus go dtí scéalaithe eile, Tomás (Mhárthain) Mac Gearailt, Tadhg Ó Guithín, Seán 'ac Gearailt ó Mhárthan a bhí pósta ar na Gorta Dubha. ('Danger' a bhí mar leasainm air seo). Peig Sayers agus a mac Maidhc (File) Ó Guithín, Domhnaill Ó Mainín ó Chill Uraidh (Domhnaillín an Deataigh) a thug an scéal is faide a scríobh sé riamh do Joe Daly, scéal a thóg dhá oíche dhéag é a scríobh síos. Ansan bhí Seán Ó Grífín ó Chathair Boilg ann. An fear deireanach acu seo ní raibh aon ainm in airde air mar scéalaí i measc an phobail mar ní bhíodh sé ag insint scéalta go poiblí toisc iarracht don luaith-bhéalaíocht a bheith air. Ach bhí a shaol caite aige istigh i dtigh Pheats 'ac Loinsigh, ag éisteacht leis go beacht agus ag tabhairt gach aon scéal acu leis, 'An Gadaí Dubh', 'Balor Béimneach', 'Cuid, Céad agus Céatach', 'Feirmeoir Aodhaire na hAimsire', etc. Faoin am go raibh Joe Daly ag bailiú scéalta bhí Peats ar shlí na fírinne ach d'aimsigh sé Seán Ó Grífín agus fuair na scéalta ar fad uaidh. Tá na scéalta sin go hiontach. Arís níorbh aon díobháil, b'fhéidir, éisteacht le Italo Calvino agus é ag trácht ar an ábhar céanna:

De réir mar a thugas faoin obair, ag tógaint ceann i gcónaí don ábhar a bhí ar fáil, á rangú agus á chatalógú, do ghaibh sórt buile mé, díocas thar meon agus gan cur suas, chun teacht ar gach sórt leagain agus malairt leagain de mhóitífeanna áirithe. Bhí sé mar a bheadh fiabhras orm a ghaibh lastuas díom. Bhraitheas go raibh paisiún orm faoi mar a bheadh ar fheithideolaí, sa tslí is go mbeinn lántsásta iomlán dá raibh scríte ag Proust a thabhairt suas ar aon leagan amháin eile den scéal úd 'Cac ór, a asailín'. [An leagan Gaeilge den scéal seo is forleithne ná an ceann darb ainm 'Cac airgead, a chapaillín bháin'.] (aistrithe ón mBéarla ag Nuala Ní Dhomhnaill)

Ba shásamh mór aigne dhom é go raibh scríbhneoir eile tar éis gabháil tríd an sórt buile a bhí orm féin. Ní hamháin san ach teacht amach ar an taobh eile. Óir ba é an tréimhse seo a chaith sé ar snámh in aigéan dosháraithe seo an bhéaloidis a chuir athrú mór foirme ar scríbhneoireacht Italo Calvino. D'fhág sé an réalachas laistiar dó agus thug aghaidh ar an rud go dtugtar anois 'meitificsean' air, mar shampla ina úrscéal iontach, *Once on a Winter's Night a Traveller*. Bhain sé cuid den mhearbhall díom é a fheiscint ag cur síos ar ar rud céanna a bhí tarlaithe domhsa. Bhí sé chomh cóngarach san do m'eispéireas féin gur dhóigh liom gur bhain sé na focail as mo bhéal:

Ar feadh dhá bhliain do mhaireas i gcoillte agus i gcaisleáin faoi dhraíocht, mé 'om stracadh idir fonn machnaimh agus fonn gníomhaíochta ... I rith an dá bhliain seo thóg an domhan mórthimpeall orm gnéithe den saol sí air féin agus gach rud a tharla ba dhraíocht nó biorán suain éigin nó claochlú de shaghas amháin nó de shaghas eile faoi ndear é ... D'oscail neadracha nathrach faoi bhonn mo chos agus chomh hobann céanna dhein sruthanna bainne is meala dhóibh. Do dhein tuismitheoirí míthrócaireacha de ríthe a cheapfá go dtí sin a bheith gan cháim. Do tháinig ríochtaí a bhí faoi gheasaibh thar n-ais ina mbeathaidh. Tuigeadh dom go raibh rialacha dearmadta shaol an bhéaloidis ag titim tóin thar cheann amach as an mboiscín draíochta a bhí oscailte agam. (aistrithe ón mBéarla ag Nuala Ní Dhomhnaill)

Agus arís, a deir sé:

Anois nó go bhfuil an leabhar críochnaithe agam, tuigtear dom nach rámhaillíocht nó speabhraídí a bhí orm dearbhú glan a dhéanamh ar rud go raibh amhras láidir agam air cheana féin, is é sin, go bhfuil an fhírinne ag roinnt le scéalta sí. (aistrithe ón mBéarla ag Nuala Ní Dhomhnaill)

Bhíos-sa tagaithe ar an tuairim chéanna go neamhspleách, agus mo dhánta athraithe ó bhonn dá bharr.

De réir mar a bhíos ag taighdeadh liom bhí mo shuim ag athrú ó rud go rud. Tar éis bheith ag gabháilt do na cóirithe catha agus do na móitífeanna idirnáisiúnta thosnaíos ag cur suime sna scéalaithe, agus go háirithe sna scéalaithe ban, daoine ar nós Peig Sayers, Cáit Ruiséal agus ach go háirithe Máire Ruiséal. Is dóigh liom gur thiteas i ngrá le Máire Ruiséal. Ní mar a chéile an cur chuige a bhí aici in aon chor agus a bhí ag Peig Sayers. Tá rud éigin geall le barócach ag baint le Peig, tá castaíocha beaga reitrice ag roinnt léi. Is maith léi focail dheacra nó 'carraigreacha' agus cuireann focal go minic scéal i gcuimhne dhi. Abraimis nuair a luaitear na prátaí ar a dtugtar 'minions' deir sí: 'Bliain na minions ab ea é nuair a bhí m'athair istigh age baile. Tháinig bean Ultach isteach 'on tigh chuige agus ...' away léi. Tá nósmhaireacht scéalaíochta ana-dhíreach ag Máire Ruiséal, cé go bhfuil cóiriú catha na scéalaíochta aici chomh maith le duine: 'Agus bhí drúcht agus deireanaí an tráthnóna agus na hoíche ag teacht uirthi, agus an madra gearra ag dul ar scáth na copóige, an chopóg ag teitheadh uaidh, agus an madra rua ag dul ina phluaisín féin, ní nach locht ar an madra macánta.'

Tá aon áit amháin i lár scéil a thaitníonn go mór liom, áit a labhrann sí i leataoibh le Joe Daly: 'Bhí clann an rí amuigh ar an ... Joe, an féidir liom an focal Béarla a úsáid anseo?' 'Abair leat,' arsa Joe. 'Bhí clann an rí amuigh ar an bpiazza ...'

Táim an-shásta a fheiscint gur roghnaigh Éilís Ní Dhuibhne scéal le Máire Ruiséal don chaibidil ar an Traidisiún Béil, sa chúigiú himleabhar de dhíolaim *The Field Day Anthology*. Tugann sí scéal darb ainm Scéal an Ghabhairín Bháin, sampla iontach de 'síscéal banúil' nó 'feminine fairytale'. Leagan is ea é den seanscéal 'Psyche agus Amor'. Ag trácht ar an méid a deir Vladimir Propp i dtaobh an scéil seo ina aiste *Historical Roots of Russian Fairy Tales*, deir Calvino:

> Although the customs of millennia are disregarded, the plot of the story still reflects the spirit of those laws and describes every love thwarted and forbidden by law, convention or social disparity. That is why it has been possible, from prehistory to the present, to preserve, not as a fixed formula but as a flowing element, the sensuality so often underlying this love, evident in the ecstasy and frenzy of mysterious nocturnal embraces.

Tá an grá collaí seo le braith ar leagan Mháire Ruiséal den scéal agus, ar chuma scéalaíocht Pheig Sayers, tá oscailteacht aigne ann i dtaobh nádúir an duine nach mbeifeá ag súil leis, b'fhéidir, ón léamh coitianta a deintear ar an mbanscéalaí mar dhealbh náisiúnta:

> Do chuadar isteach i gcúirt bhreá. Do labhair sé léi ansan: 'Mhuise, sea anois,' ar seisean, 'cé acu is fearr leatsa anois,' ar seisean, 'mise bheith mar ghabhar istoíche is mar fhear isló nó mar fhear istoíche agus mar ghabhar isló?' 'Ó go deimhin,' ar sise, 'is fearr liom cuideachta na hoíche – tú bheith mar fhear istoíche agus id ghabhar isló.' Mar sin do bhí. ('Scéal an Ghabhairín Bháin', ó bhéalaithris Mháire Ruiséal, RBÉ 243:162)

Thugas faoi ndeara de réir mar a chuas isteach sa Roinn le Béaloideas gur athraigh mo shuim. Le déanaí is sna píosaí beaga seanchais is mó a chuirim spéis, na scéalta beaga neafaiseacha a thit amach do dhaoine. Sítheach Baile Eaglaise ag cur síos ar cé méid tigh a leagadh i ngach baile fearainn le linn an Droch-Shaoil. Peats Dhónail (Ó Cíobháin) na Muirí ag caint ar iascach nó ar Thomás na bPúcaí, gaol dom fhéin. Bhí scéal amháin aige i dtaobh Thomáis agus caithfead é a bhréagnú. Bhí triúr ban óg ag gabháilt aniar ag an am céanna ar an Leataoibh Meánach. Bhí fios ag Tomás na bPúcaí, agus dúirt sé go mbeadh púir mhór ar an mbaile ach ní déarfadh sé cioca duine de na mná óga a scuabfaí. Mar a tharla ba í an bhean ba mhó go raibh gaol aige léi a scuabadh, bean mic a dheirféar. Cailleadh í den fhiabhras aerach tar éis di leanbh iníne a thabhairt ar an saol. 'Agus,' arsa Peats Dhónail, 'cailleadh an bhean óg go luath ina dhiaidh sin, agus cailleadh an iníon chomh maith' (ó bhéalaithris Pheats Dhónail (Ó Cíobháin), RBÉ). Bhuel, níor cailleadh an iníon. Conas go bhfuil a fhios agam san? Mar ba í mo mháthair chríonna í, agus mura mbeadh sí siúd tar éis maireachtaint, ní bheinnse anseo anois.

Scéal eile a bhain le mo mhuintir féin a d'úsáideas mar réamhrá le mo chnuasach deireanach, *Cead Aighnis*:

Trí Anam an Duine

Bhíos istigh sa leabaidh im' chodhladh theas i mBaile Móir agus pé rud a thug Eoghainín Finton amach chonaic sé ag gabháil amach as an dtigh mé. Ghlaoigh sé ar a bhean, Léan Ní Chearna. 'Hanamain diabhal, a Léan,' ar seisean, 'tá stróc nó rud éigin ar Sheán! Féach taobh aon tí síos é. Téir amach,' ar seisean 'agus glaoigh air.' Ach chonaic sé a' casadh aríst mé agus ag dul isteach 'on tigh. Ach níor ghlaoigh Léan in aon chor orm. Ach bhíodar á rá liom lárna mháireach agus ní chreidfinn in aon Eoghainín mara mbeadh Léan á rá. Dúrt leis nár fhágas an leaba ó chuas inti gur fhágas ar maidin í, ach mé im' chodhladh go sámh. 'Bíonn a leithéid i gceist,' arsa Léan, 'agus do chuimhníos-sa air. Dá nglaofainnse an uair sin air,' arsa Léan, 'd'fhanfadh sé ann go deo.'

Ach táim á chlos riamh go bhfuil an duine ina thrí chuid. Tá an t-anam anála ann, an t-anam mothála agus an t-anam síoraíochta.

Fanfaidh an t-anam síoraíochta ionat go dtí go gcaillfear tú. N'fheadar ab é an t-anam anála nó an t-anam mothála liomsa a bhí lasmuigh agus mé im' chodladh. N'fheadar é sin.' (Ó bhéalaithris Sheáin Uí Chíobháin, RBÉ 965: 63)

Ach chun filleadh ar an scéal a bhí agam i dtús na cainte seo, i dtaobh 'laincisí síoda a bheith ar chaoire na Cathrach', bhíos istigh sa Roinn le Béaloideas an lá cheana agus thángas de sheans ar eolas breise ina thaobh. Tuigeadh domhsa riamh gur eachtra miotaseolaíochta a bhí i gceist leis seo. Sampla suaithinseach ab ea é dar liom de chumas filíochta na muintire agus den chumas iontach samhlaíochta a bhí riamh le braith go láidir i gCorca Dhuibhne. Níor taibhsíodh riamh dom go raibh aon bhonn stairiúil aige, ach féach go bhfuil. Bád mór seoil darb ainm an *Lady Nelson* ab ea é a raiceáladh ar an Sceilg agus í lán de phíopaí fíona i dteannta an tsíoda. Is i ndiaidh an long seo a raiceáil ann a thógadar an teach solais sa Sceilg:

Oíche cheoigh ab ea é agus bhí an captaen a' rá go rabhadar trí léig ó aon talamh. Bhí cuid den gcriú ar a mhalairt de thuairim, agus an ceart acu mar ní fada nó gur bhuail sí an Sceilg. Briseadh agus báthadh agus bascadh a raibh innti ach triúr a chuaigh in airde ar smut adhmaid. Tháinig a dó nó trí de laethanta ceoigh is báisteach aniar is aneas is bhí na píopaí fíona ag gluaiseacht aniar. Bhíodh báid ag dul á gcuardach. Bhí Cuan Fionntrá lán de bháid agus Cathair a' Treanntaigh. Bhí fear darb ainm Scainlin agus bád aige is a chriú siar sa bhá ag lorg an fhíona nuair a chonaiceadar an raic i bhfad uathu is na fir anáirde air. Beirt a bhí ann nuair a shroiseadar iad. Bhí fear eile tamaillín beag roimis sin taréis titim san uisce le codladh. Thógadar an bheirt is do shábháileadar iad. Sin ar tháinig saor. Chuireadar crann is dhá sheol chun Scainlin is a chriú mar bhuíochas ina dhiaidh sin.

Tá súil agam go bhfuilim tar éis léaspairt éigin a thabhairt daoibh, ar cad é chomh tábhachtach domhsa is atá béaloideas na hÉireann

[92]

agus bailiúcháin an Choimisiún Béaloideasa, ach go háirithe. Is dóigh liom go n-oibríonn sé ar dhá leibhéal, leibhéal na Gaeilge ar dtúis, áit a gcuireann sé i gcuimhne dhom an dlús is an neafais teangan a chuala á chaitheamh thar bhuailtí ó dhuine go duine is mé im' leanbh. Ansan oibríonn sé ar leibhéal na samhlaíochta, nuair a thugann móitífeanna na scéalta agus fiú na píosaí beaga seanchais atá scaipthe anso is ansúd ar fuaid na lámhscríbhinne samhlaoidí iontacha dom gur féidir liom bheith ag imirt leo, ag spraoi agus ag gleáchas, á gcaitheamh san aer is ag breith orthu arís. Agus ar ndóigh is é an spraoi sin ceann de na riachtanais is tábhachtaí in obair chruthaitheach.

Tá rud amháin eile a theastaíonn uaim a lua sara dtagaim go deireadh mo chuid cainte anocht, agus baineann sé sin le teideal na cainte, 'neacha neamhbheo agus nithe nach bhfuil ann'. Bhuel, go dtí le déanaí do thabharfainn an leabhar go raibh a leithéid de theideal ar cheann de na rannaíocha atá sa chatalóg ghinearálta sa Roinn le Béaloideas Éireann, seo catalóg a bhí déanta amach ag duine de bhunaitheoiri na roinne, an bailitheoir Seán Ó Súilleabháin. Ach mo léir, nuair a chuas á chuardach i gcomhair na cainte seo ní fhéadfainn í a fháil. Do chuardaíos is do chuardaíos is ní bhfuaireas aon rian de in aon chor, rud a thugann i gceist go bhfuil seans maith nach raibh sé riamh ann agus gur speabhraídí a bhí ormsa ina thaobh ó thus deiridh. Tharlódh sé.

Ba mhaith liom an focal deireanach a thabhairt do Ghearóid Ó Crualaoich ó *Leabhar na Caillí, The Book of the Cailleach: Stories of the Wise-Woman Healer.* Tá píosa den chaibidil 'Traidisiún agus Teoiric' a léimeann chun mo shúile ar an bpointe boise mar gurb é atá á rá ag Gearóid ná an méid a bhíos ag iarraidh a chur in iúil sa léacht seo:

The texts of the oral narrative presented in this book and the commentaries offered with them bear witness, hopefully, to the way that traditional material, frequently seen as outmoded, naïve, parochially-bound, can constitute a rich imaginative resource for our own times and our own circumstances in a world where the local and the global are intermeshing at an increased rate for greater numbers and in ways not previously imagined.

Agus sin tús agus deireadh mo scéil – an chuma ina bhfuil acmhainn iontach againn in oideas béil na hÉireann, pioctha ó lámh-scríbhinní na Roinne anseo, nó ó ghnáthchaint scéalaithe maithe, ar chuma an dá dhlúthdhiosca ón mBab Feirtéar a tháinig amach anuraidh agus go raibh ráchairt chomh mór san orthu, gur dóigh liom go bhfuil siad díolta amach faoi dhó.

Níl suim ar bith agamsa réimsí teangan ná eiseamláirí litríochta a thabhairt isteach sa Ghaeilge – *per se* – cé go raghaidh mé ar thóir foclóir eolaíochta, fisice nó ceimice, má tá gá agam leis, mar shampla nuair a theastaíonn uaim cur síos ar an bhfeiniméan nádúrtha san An Chaor Aduaidh a chonac uair gur thugas turas ar Fairbanks Alasca. Ach an rud a theastaíonn uaimse a dhéanamh thar aon ní eile ná rud éigin a chur ar fáil trí bhíthin acmhainní nádúrtha na teangan nach raibh san fhilíocht roimhe sin, in aon teanga. Is chuige sin a bhím ag póirseáil liom sa Roinn le Béaloideas, agus le cúnamh na ndéithe agus na ndeamhan, na neach neamhbheo agus na nithe nach bhfuil ann, beidh mé á dhéanamh an dá lá is an fhaid a mhairfidh mé.

DEIREADH NA LÉACHTA ANSEO. A BHUÍ LE DIA.

Tras-scríbhinn de léacht a tugadh sa Choláiste Ollscoile, Baile Átha Cliath, i mí Dheireadh Fómhair 2003.

The Hag, the Fair Maid and the Otherworld

I wrote a poem recently.

Primavera

Everything changed when *she* passed by.
I tell you, she would make the grey stones cry for joy.
Small birds that had till then been cowed
opened their throats and piped up, loud
as a minstrel's fife, as if they couldn't
care less if they had a note in their heads or not.
Wildflowers that had been so humble, so shy
in asking for a place on the edges of flowerbeds
now jostle for elbowroom. Look! The scarlet pimpernel
blinds me suddenly with its crimson starbursts.

Me? I was weeping softly on a branch,
hidden under a fig-leaf, in a huff,
pretty cheesed off with life.
It would take much more than a smile
from some comely maid to entice *me* from my shell.
(That much I had announced to one and all.)
But she did it. With one flick of her wrist,
with one joyful, proud glance over her shoulder,
she tugged at the very roots within me and left me without
a leg to stand on, my head spinning, restless and on edge.

Trans. Caoimhín Mac Giolla Léith

I should have called it 'Anois Teacht an Earraigh' (the name of Raftery's poem on spring), but at the same time I was thinking of two paintings by Botticelli – *Spring* and *The Birth of Venus*. And so, in the end, I called the poem 'Primavera'. I could have equally called it 'Fair Maid' or 'Hag/Fair Maid'. It would make sense and would bring me back into the Gaelic tradition, both the literary and the folkloric. This double image of the fair maiden and the hag is as old in Ireland as the literature itself. As to the literary tradition, one needs but mention the story from Old Irish in which Niall of the Nine Hostages lies with the old hag at the bottom of the well and she is instantly transformed into a fair maid. 'I am Sovereignty,' she says, and she prophesises that Niall and his descendants will be kings of Ireland.

In the *aisling* we find some of the most beautiful and compelling poems in the canon – from 'Gile na Gile' to 'Róisín Dubh', to 'Úr-Chill an Chreagáin' – and Irish literature would be much the poorer without them. Indeed, where would English literature in Ireland be without 'Oh my Dark Rosaleen' and: 'Did you see an old woman going down the road?' 'I didn't, but I saw a young girl and she had the walk of a queen,' not to mention other examples of the same thing such as the bride who leaps on the back of the main character in Stewart Parker's play *Northern Star*. I happened to be at the local hairdresser when that play was staged in Dublin, overhearing my neighbours as they chatted about this and that. One of the women began to talk about the play she had seen the night before: 'And as soon as I saw that jilted bride I knew who she was,' she said. 'She was Ireland.'

But it was the old tradition that I was more interested in and it was from the mouths of people that I first came across the image of the hag. There was an old woman once by the name of Mór in Dún Chaoin and there were loads of stories about her as I was growing up. She constantly quarrelled with her husband Donncha Dí, and one day he lost patience with her and prayed for the length and breadth of Ireland between them. This happened in the twinkle of an eye and he was taken up into the air and landed up in Donaghadee in County Down – and he's been there ever since. Years later I was listening to Breandán Feirtéar on Raidió na Gaeltachta interviewing Hannah Daly, former postmistress of Dún Chaoin. They were discussing Mór and what had happened to her husband and then Hannah said nonchalantly: 'There were some people outside Callaghan's on a Saturday evening and they saw him going east with a bundle on his back.' As though it only happened yesterday or today. I had to laugh. Nothing would satisfy me but to write a poem in which that line occurred and this I did some time afterwards:

Closure

... and then
one day
the god departed.

He rose up with the dawning of the day,
Took his razor, his toothbrush and his overnight case
And did a runner.
People outside Callaghan's in Dingle
On Saturday afternoon saw him heading east
A pack on his back.

I heard him passing too, though as if
In a dream, a voice
Singing and a scatter of notes on the whistle
Like the sound of oboes within the stage
'Tis the god Hercules, whom Anthony loved
now leaves him –

Now I am empty, and this space within me –
I can't tell what might fill it
Or how. If I might follow him
On that perilous byway
Dishevelled, with shoes untied ...
But the length and breadth of Ireland I can't walk over.

Trans. Eiléan Ní Chuilleanáin

Of course when I was thinking about the Mór story, I remembered another one about her and used that as well. According to this tale Mór became lonesome after Donncha and she travelled to the top – or the bottom – of Ireland looking for him. She left her own house in Dún Chaoin, and when she came to Barr an Chlasaigh and saw the wide and beautiful parish of Ventry extending before her, she became afraid: 'Oh, the length and breadth of Ireland!' she said, and turned back home. There is another story concerning this adventure. On the road home nature called and she did a piss by the side of the ditch. It was such a powerful stream that it formed two grooves on both sides of the road, which give it its placename today. My aunt's husband, Thomas Murphy, used '*Leá bumbóire*' or '*Leá múin Móire*' as an expression or as a curse, tongue-in-cheek, and he'd have no respect for you if you weren't able to understand the saying, or tell the story that went with it.

This is an example of the significance attached to the image of the hag in the mind of the people and in the nature of their folklore. It is especially true in the case of placenames and their lore. We'd be here all week listing townlands and lowlands and highlands and lakes named after the hag or associated with her. This tradition is older than the Celtic era, it must be said. Gearóid Ó Crualoich states in his *The Book of the Cailleach*:

> Old Europe was intensified in Ireland, where an abiding sense of a supreme, sovereign, female, cosmic agency appears to have operated on the incoming culture to a degree that resulted in a continuing, powerful sensibility to the presence in the landscape of such divine, female agency – a sensibility that has remained at the heart of Irish ancestral cosmology and mythological legend.

I have always been interested in this particular image. One can see it in the first poems I wrote, poems that I can call poems other than compositions in verse:

Donnacha Di's Testimony

She stood naked
in the dark,
her palms cold
like luminous fish
on my shoulders:
her hips
flashing fire
beneath the two moons
of her breasts.
  I sank my head
  in her sea-weed hair
  and bitter waves of sea
  bruised and battered me,
  our white-horse waves
  rusted to rats:
  all became empurpled.
In the morning waking
my head aching
I saw sallow scales encrusted her
and rotten teeth from the abyss
snarled at me and hissed.
I took my awl and last
and left the place fast!

Trans. Michael Hartnett

Every time I come across a trace of the hag, she sparks off a poem in me.
This is a relatively recent example:

Eithne the Hun

The earliest woman to be cited
in that mighty tome of Keating –

The Growth of Learning in Ireland –
figured children were for eating.

She'd been fostered out, seemingly,
with the Decies tribe of Munster
who reared her on a diet
of the fatted flesh of youngsters

so as to bring on her menarche
before she was well ready
and get land they were promised
out of the blade who might wed her:

but the lamb must still be waiting
to be led to the altar
by the mess they've just made
of those three in Gibraltar.

Trans. Medbh McGuckian

A couple of years ago when the writer and publisher Micheál Ó Conghaile gave the Ó Cadhain Lecture here in UCD, he said he was in two minds about it. He'd much prefer, he said, to write a short story, or attempt one – even if it never got finished. I am in the same situation. Every time I sat down to write this lecture, I started writing a poem instead. Nothing to complain about – we should never refuse the Muse when she comes our way. You could be waiting quite a while for inspiration to come and it might not come at all.

I have always been fascinated by folklore, though I wouldn't always have called it by such a lofty name. What were they but little stories stitched into the everyday narratives around me, a five-year-old exile, back in my aunty Máire's house in Cathair an Treantaigh in the parish of Ventry in the mid-fifties. Little things that happened from day to day, an old story or an unusual reference attached to them. Like the day a few years later when I as a young girl was walking up the Cathair Road in a silk dress made of two pieces of material that were stitched together with a hem below – the first and only bit of sewing I ever did. 'Oh,' said John Sé, a cousin of my grandfather's who met me on the road, 'I like your dress.' 'Yes,' says I with great pride, ''tis silk.' 'Don't I know it well,' says John Sé, 'there was so much silk in the place they call Silk Cliff that the people of the parish were tying their animals with it: "The sheep of the Cathair had fetters of silk," as the poet said.' A sentence that will stay in my head forever and that would leap out at me years later when I was writing a poem.

Not only that but my aunt's husband, Tomás Ó Murchú, or Thomas Murphy as he was better known, was by the fireside with me. He was a man with a vast knowledge of the parish and of the lore of the seven old parishes west of Dingle. I heard him one night in Dónall Ó Catháin's pub when Breandán Mac Gearailt convened Oireachtas na nGael in Ballyferriter. Máirtín Ó Cadhain was in the company. Tomás and Art Ó Beoláin differed about the location and the construction of the Carraig chapel:

> 'It's built on Carraig,' says Art.
> 'The divil it is,' says Tomás, 'it's built on Bóthar Buí.'
> 'It's built on Carraig,' says Art again.
> 'Who told you that?' says Tomás.
> 'Haven't I read it? It's written in the book.'
> 'Oh,' says Tomás, 'whoever wrote that book he put down a divil of lies in it!'
> 'You can't beat him,' says Máirtín Ó Cadhain, 'you can't beat the proper native speaker.'

Around that time I gave a copy of the book *Romantic Hidden Kerry* to Tomás. A couple of days later I went enquiring. 'Well, Tomás, what's your opinion of the book?' 'It's not bad,' he says, 'it goes back two hundred years. Not bad – but I'd go the four for you.'

This was no great exaggeration because he knew that it was big guns from a ship in Dingle Bay, and not in Ventry Harbour as one might expect, that knocked the top off the town castle, Caisleán na dTreantach. There wasn't a stone upon stone of that castle to be seen in a hundred years. It's likely that it was in the time of Dún an Óir, or at the latest during the Cromwellite wars that the court fell. There hadn't been any of the Treantaigh in the Dingle Peninsula in a long, long time – although they gave their names to three townlands in the parish of Ventry and the name is still common enough in North Kerry. They didn't flourish as much as their fellow Normans in the peninsula, the Ferriters, the Rices, the Gearaltaighs and the Husseys.

Tomás could go back to seven generations of his people. He had all their names and knew much about their lives. He claimed his grandfather was born in Cuan Uachtair, a village saved from the potato blight of the Great Famine. Much good it did to the tenants, because the village and two other villages in the harbour, Cuan Íochtair and Cúilín Bhán, were cleared in 1867 by Lord Cork's steward, a Cork man by the name of Leahy. Tomás always said that his grandfather was twelve years of age when they left. Many of the tenants went to America or to Fán or to the Oileán Tiar (in the Blaskets) or were scattered through-out the district. Some of them came to Cathair. 'How did they manage to settle down in Cathair?' says I. 'Wasn't the place deserted,' says he, 'everyone had gone away.'

He knew how the chapel in the parish of Ventry was transferred from its old site in the eastern part of the parish, where the school now is, to the site in Imleach Shlat, given away for nothing by Muintir Shé of Imleach. His granduncle Micheál, who tragically died after going to America, was the last person prayed for in the old chapel and his aunt was the first to be baptised in the new one. He knew a lot about my own people, stuff you wouldn't want to hear sometimes. 'Léan with the puss on her and the scald crow's eye,' he called my great-grandmother, Léan Ní Chearna. It was when I was becoming more interested in Irish as a young girl that I began to take down much of this lore from him, but my memories of him, and of many others, go back further still. They had the sharp tongues and wouldn't blink before cutting you down a bit if they wanted to: '*Leá bumbóire*' or '*Leá múin Móire to you*' was a frequent expression, or curse I should say, and another: 'What would you know, it's not that you have the origins of all stories.'

But my memories stretch back further than that to the period I spent with them as a five-year-old 'orphan' over from England. I remember the time when Johnny Long and his son Maidhc were farming next door, and Jacksaí Sé and his sister Neil were up beyond them in the village. John Sé's house was at the top of the village and the pump in their yard was famous for never drying out in the summer. Each man of them would stand on his own little hill throwing all sorts of daggered phrases at the next man. I can't recall a single sentence now but I remember the speech as being eloquent and poetic. Little wonder then that when I first began to write poetry I drew my linguistic resources from them:

Mór Anguished

Mór, firmly under lock and key
in her own tiny mind
(2" x 4" x 3")
of grey, pinkish stuff
(here be the wounds
that drown the flies
while other flies survive
to make their maggots
on the carrion fringe).

'Listen, in God's name,' she begs
the magpies and the crows
that come at evening
to upset their guts,
'every one's enclosed
in their own tiny hells.'

The small birds
scatter and spread
when she flings up at them
a sod of earth

Trans. Michael Hartnett

There were others in the village who had the great talk. Not only were they native speakers, they were the finest of speakers too. The most Gaelic of them all, Tomás Mhairéad (Ó Sé) died in 1956, a year exactly before my arrival. He was the last monoglot. They say he had no English. I don't know if I ever believed that entirely. 'How could he have no English living here with all the coastguards around for more than a hundred years?' 'He kept away from them. He didn't mix with them.' There might have been a bit of politics involved as well. He was one of those who attended the first public meeting of the Land League during the Land War, a meeting held in two hundred or so *navogues* (curraghs) in the middle of the harbour when Lord Cork wouldn't allow the meeting on land. His people were known as the Parnells for many a day. But if he wasn't there for me there were many more who were: Fitzie, John Sé, Jacksaí and his sister Neil, Joeín and Annie Sheehy and her brother Jackie, Johnny Long and his son Maidhc Long na Cathrach. They were there in plenty, and they were honey-tongued.

Other things were happening in my life and I got the hell out of Ireland as quickly as I could. After spending seven years abroad, mostly in the Netherlands and Turkey, I knew that what I most wanted in the world was to return to Ireland and start writing full time. I applied for and received a bursary from the Arts Council. This allowed me to come home with my two children and settle in my people's summer house in Cathair an Treantaigh. My children were so fair that we were known as 'Nuala and the White Turkeys'. I was trying my hand at everything: a novel in which I got bogged down, a selection of short stories that was finished but never published, but, above all, I sank myself into poetry. My husband hadn't arrived yet and I was very lonely in the house on my own with the children asleep looking out over Ventry Strand and the ebbed tide. It was in folkloric terms that I expressed myself and invoked the persona of a mermaid:

The Mermaid

'Ebbtide' I said,
'the tide will have to turn
and cover this waste of sand,
pour over limpets on rocks
over wrack drying waterless
(ribbons like withered vellum)
because the lugworms' faeces
make me nauseous.'

Floodtide ebbtide
floodtide ebbtide
rise and fall
rise and fall
the same again.
Everything's so bad now
it can't get worse
but 'we have ways of making you talk'
I hear in Gestapo accents
(water goes down and down
But no tide nears me).

Though I've got a fish's tail
I'm not unbeautiful:
my hair is long and yellow
and there's a shine from my scales
you won't see on landlocked women.
Their eyes are like stones

but look into these eyes of mine
and you will see the sturgeon
and you will see fine seals
gambolling in my pupils

Not without pain
have I landed:
I broke
the natural law.
I swapped swimming
for walking on earth,
picking my steps
like a curlew.
Believe you me
it was love, not God,
who gave the order.

You left
and took my magic cap.
It's not as easy to get back
in the roof's rafters
as it was in the fable.
I dug to the subsoil
and saw no sign of it.
The tide also fails us
and a rat
gnaws at the very sun.

Trans. Michael Hartnett

Around the same time Seán Ó Tuama introduced me to Joe Daly and Bab Feirtéar. I'd visit them often and they were very good to me. They were great company. Bab in her house, a grand fire in the hearth, cups of tea going round, and Joe and his wife Peig in their house or in Daniel's pub in Ballyferriter. I remember taping some stories from Bab and I'd play them to myself in bed until sleep came. It's no exaggeration to say that they influenced me greatly. Not only did they supply me with titles and narrative frameworks for my first two books of poems, they also taught me how to make something more universal out of the raw emotions and changing circumstances of my own life. The lore helped me to tell stories with a slant, as Emily Dickinson once recommended: 'Tell the truth, but tell it slant', and to say things that could not be expressed directly.

An example of this approach is the title poem of my second volume, 'Féar Suaithinseach'. The first time I taped Bab, she gave me a version of the story on which I based my poem. It wasn't long on tape, however, before my sister destroyed it by taping pop music over it – she had mistaken it for a blank tape because there was nothing on it but speech.

I went back to Bab and got another and then another version, but the version on which the poem was based was gone. As it happens, she never told it again the way I first remembered it: the way the priest would handle the communion so deftly. That was the expression I needed above all other tellings. The version I eventually used was the one I was given by Professor Bo Almqvist, a taped version later transcribed by Dr Ríonach Uí Ógáin. By this time other great changes were happening in my life. We had spent three years in Corca Dhuibhne. For one of these years my husband had been working in Dublin, visiting us every second weekend. We knew that the journey was too hard for him and that we would have to move to Dublin. It was horrible to be torn away from the western world and for a long time I missed the Gaeltacht sorely. I had Raidió na Gaeltachta on all the time, and for many years afterwards I contributed an insert on Maidhc Sé's programme about local history, especially from my gleanings in the Department of Folklore. It was Joe Daly who pointed me towards the Department in the first place. He told me to go in, that it would do me good, and, he said to me, 'See what you see.'

Firstly I traced my own people, beginning of course with Thomas Murphy – and yes, he was there. He had contributed three stories. One story was a great wonder, the story of the boy and the holy pictures, and the beginning of a story called 'The Mouse and the Wren'. Joe had told me that the story would be there. It's a story to be found in *Seanchaí Muimhneach*, collected by Pádraig Ó Siochfhradha, or 'An Seabhac' as he was known, at the beginning of the century. By the time Joe started collecting in the thirties and forties, it was no longer in the memories or on the lips of the people. He picked up fragments of the story here and there, but no one had its beginning. He came down to Cathair an Treantaigh to find it because he had heard it might be there. Thomas had it. According to the description at the beginning of the story he had heard it from his mother twenty-odd years before. He describes himself as the son of a farmer, twenty-eight years of age. That was true, since he had not yet been given the land from his father.

But the father himself, Peats Ó Murchú, was the biggest jewel I discovered. I had always heard a good deal about Peats, as someone who was a very fine speaker, and in my own time people used many of his phrases. For example, his son Tomás was born on a night of snow so they called him ever afterwards 'Tomáisín an tSneachta' ('Little Tom of the Snow'). The day after his birth Peats went walking past Mám na Gaoithe and up Bóthar na Leataithe on his way north to Cathair Deargáin where his wife Cáit Foley came from. It was a snowy day, the Feast of the Epiphany, and my granny, a young girl in Leataoibh Meánach, was throwing snowballs at her friends. He was greeted with 'Any news, Peats?' 'I have,' said he, 'a son last night, the makings of a giant. He has the bones of a young horse and never will he get a cold.'

He was right about the second half because Tomás always had good health and he came through the Great Flu of 1918 without a bother when three coffins – two uncles and a brother – were taken out of the house within a fortnight. The first part of the prophecy wasn't up to much, however, because although he was supple and active into his old age he was far from being a giant. He always admired a good physique: 'Nothing like it,' he'd say. My granny always said she little thought when she was growing up that she would have a daughter who would marry the child of that snowy night.

Another expression that stayed in people's minds was the agitation on Peats when he was bargaining with a man at a fair in Dingle. 'Such pride from a man,' said he, 'with only two worthless beasts compared to the man with eight cows in a city,' referring of course to himself.

But it was only when I saw all that Joe Daly had collected from Peats that I understood what a fine *seanchaí* we had in him. He had the long stories of the Fenian Lays, the story of Balor Béimneach, the story of Fionn and King Athadonas. Not only that but he had the battle rhetoric as well: the battle rhetoric of the warrior, the battle rhetoric of the vessel, the battle rhetoric of the sea. For a while I was very taken with the battle rhetoric:

'Which would you prefer,' said the giant, 'hard piercing wrestling or the clash of sharp steel swords on each other's ribs?' 'I'd prefer the hard piercing wrestling because it is such that I practised on the greens with the sons of noblemen.' And they set to it with downward blows and upward blows and with wrestling holds at one another and he who would come from the bottom of the world to the top of the world to view two wrestlers, it is these two he should be watching and the hard ground softened under them and the soft ground hardened and hollows became hills and hills became hollows. From the grey stones beneath them they drew up wells of pure water and through the hard sods scattering here, there, and everywhere beneath their feet, they would extract three teeth from the hag that sits over in the city of London and she reddening her pipe, and those three teeth would not stop in their course through mountain and moor before they toppled three courts yonder in the Eastern world. (From the telling of Pádraig Ó Murchú, NFC 475: 602–3)

I took it all in. It became a bit of a frenzy. I went from one *seanchaí* to another, checking different versions of the battle rhetoric. Peats a' tSaoir 'ac Loinsigh from Baile an tSléibhe had the best of them. He had given stories to the American collector Jeremiah Curtin as a young man below in Ard an Bhóthair. He told the stories in Irish and his father put English on them for Curtin. But Peats wasn't in the least bit satisfied with the English version. When he was reciting them again into an ediphone for the collector Seán Ó Dubhda, he said:

> I was telling stories for Curtin and his wife was writing them down and my father was putting English on the Irish for her and a boy, a farmer's son, didn't he buy one of those books and my stories were in it and you wouldn't believe it, he wasn't putting them down in any proper way at all. The battle rhetoric wasn't in it at all. They weren't able to write the battle rhetoric at all, at all! (From the telling of Peats a' tSaoir 'ac Loinsigh, RBÉ)

Is it any wonder that the poems I was writing at the time are full of all sorts of battle rhetoric? It is what came to mind as I was nursing a child and trying to describe the type of world a newborn baby comes into, a world full of sights and sounds that she could not distinguish from one another, that world of pre-symbolic sound or the chora as the feminist theorist from France, Julia Kristeva, calls it:

Feeding a Child

From honey-dew of milking
from cloudy heat of beestings
the sun rises up the back
of bare hills,
a guinea gold
to put in your hand,
my own.

You drink your fill from my breast
and fall back asleep
into a lasting dream
laughter in your face.

what is going through your head
you who are but
a fortnight on earth?

Do you know day from night
that the great early ebb
announces spring tide?
That the boats
are on deep ocean,
where live the seals and fishes
and the great whales,
and are coming hand over hand
each by seven oars manned?
That your small boat swims
óró in the bay
with the flippered peoples
and the small sea-creatures
she slippery-sleek
from stem to bow
stirring sea-sand up
sinking sea-foam down.

Trans. Michael Hartnett

There were other poems of the battle rhetoric as well, such as 'The Race'. What happened here is that I wanted to describe the wild dash of a cart race up the country. It was the battle rhetoric of the hero that I used to give that great spin to it:

Like a mad lion, like a wild bull, like one
of the crazy pigs in the Fenian cycle
or the hero leaping upon the giant
with his fringe of swinging silk,
I drive at high speed through
the small midland towns of Ireland,

catching up with the wind ahead
while the wind behind me whirls and dies.

Like a shaft from a bow, like a shot from a gun
or a sparrow-hawk in a sparrow-throng
on a March day, I scatter the road-signs,
miles or kilometres what do I care.
Nenagh, Roscrea, Mountmellick,
I pass through them in a daze;
they are only speed limits put there
to hold me up on my way to you.

Through mountain cleft, bogland and wet pasture
I race impetuously from west to east –
a headlong flight in your direction,
a quick dash to be with you.
The road rises and falls before me,
the surface changing from grit to tar;
I forget geography, all I know
is the screech of brakes and the gleam of lights.

Trans. Derek Mahon

Around the same time I came across the book *Italian Folktales*, selected and retold by Italo Calvino. This is an English translation of a collection of fairytales translated initially into Italian by Italo Calvino from the various languages of Italy. I took particular notice of what he had to say in the introduction about what happened to him when he became embroiled in the world of the fairytale:

> … it was a leap in the dark, a plunge into an unknown sea into which others before me, over the course of 150 years, had flung themselves, not out of any desire for the unusual, but because of a deep-rooted conviction that some essential, mysterious element lying in the ocean depths must be salvaged to ensure the survival of the race …

From what he had written, I knew that I was not the only one who had come down with this disease. Calvino says:

> I, however, plunged into that submarine world totally unequipped, without even a tankful of intellectual enthusiasm for anything spontaneous and primitive. I was subjected to all the discomforts of immersion in an almost formless element which, like the sluggish and passive oral tradition, could never be brought under conscious control.

I myself had moved on from battle rhetoric and Fenian lays to fairytales and to other storytellers: Tomás (Mhárthain) Mac Gearailt, Tadhg Ó Guithín, Seán 'ac Gearailt from Márthain who had married into the Gorta Dubha (nicknamed 'Danger'), Peig Sayers and her son Maidhc (File) Ó Guithín, Domhnall Ó Mainín from Cill Uraidh (Domhnaillín an Deataigh), from whom Joe Daly took the longest story ever, a story that took twelve nights to write down. Then there was Seán Ó Grífín from Cathair Boilg – he did not have a reputation as a storyteller in the community because he didn't recite stories in public, his speech being indistinct. But he had spent his life inside the house of Peats 'ac Loinsigh, carefully listening to every story and remembering them: 'An Gadaí Dubh', 'Balor Béimneach', 'Cuid, Céad agus Ceatach', 'Feirmeoir Aodhaire na hAimsire', and so on. By the time Joe Daly was collecting stories, Peats had gone to his eternal reward, but he discovered Seán Ó Grífín and got all the stories from him. Those stories are wonderful. Italo Calvino discourses on the same subject:

> Meanwhile, as I started to work, to take stock of the material available, to classify the stories into a catalog which kept expanding, I was gradually possessed by a kind of mania, an insatiable hunger for more and more versions and variants. Collating, categorizing, comparing became a fever. I could feel myself succumbing to a passion akin to that of entomologists, which I thought characteristic of the scholars of the Folklore Fellows Communications of Helsinki,

a passion which rapidly degenerated into a mania, as a result of which I would have given all of Proust in exchange for a new variant of the 'golddung donkey'. [The Irish version of this, *Cac airgead, a chapaillín bháin* or 'Shit money, little white horse', is a well-known variant.]

It gave me great satisfaction to know that another writer had experienced the same intoxication as I had. Not only that, but to have come through, because the period Calvino spent swimming in the unconquerable tide of folklore brought about great formal changes in his writing. He left realism behind and embraced metafiction, as in, for example, the wonderful novel, *Once on a Winter's Night a Traveller*. Describing what had happened to him was so close to my own experience that he took the words out of my mouth:

> For two years I have lived in woodlands and enchanted castles, torn between contemplation and action ... and during these two years the world about me gradually took on the attributes of fairyland, where everything that happened was a spell or a metamorphosis, where individuals, plucked from the chiaroscuro of a state of mind, were carried away by predestined loves, or were bewitched ... snake pits opened up and were transformed into rivers of milk; kings who had been thought kindly turned out to be brutal parents; silent, bewitched kingdoms suddenly came back to life. I had the impression that the lost rules which govern the world of folklore were tumbling out of the magic box I had opened.

And again he says:

> Now that the book is finished, I know that this was not a hallucination, a sort of professional malady, but the confirmation of something I had already suspected – folktales are real.

I had come to the same conclusion independently and my poems changed fundamentally as a consequence.

[114]

As I continued searching, my interests jumped from one thing to another. Having been immersed in battle rhetoric and international motifs, I now became interested in the storytellers themselves, especially women storytellers, the likes of Peig Sayers, Cáit Ruiséal and Máire Ruiséal in particular. I think I fell in love with Máire Ruiséal. Her approach was much different to that of Peig Sayers. Peig is almost baroque with her little rhetorical flourishes. She likes difficult words and a word can often trigger off a story in her memory. For instance when mention is made of the potatoes known as 'minions', she says, 'It was the year of the minions when my father was at home. A wild woman came into the house and ...' off she goes on her narrative. Máire Ruiséal's narrative custom was much more direct though she has as much rhetoric as anybody else: 'And the dew of late evening descended on her and night fell and the terrier was going under the dockleaf and the dockleaf was fleeing it and the fox was going into its own little den and who would blame him.'

There's one place in the middle of the story when she talks aside to Joe Daly: 'The King's children were out on the ... Joe, can I use an English word here?' 'Keep going,' says Joe. 'The King's children were out on the piazza ...'

I'm delighted that Éilís Ní Dhuibhne selected a tale from Máire Ruiséal for the chapter on Oral Tradition in the fifth volume of *The Field Day Anthology*. The story is 'Scéal an Ghabhairín Bháin' ('The Story of the White Kid Goat'), a fine example of the so-called feminine fairytale. It is a version of the ancient tale, 'Psyche and Amor'. Calvino says of it, in the context of an essay by Vladimir Propp in *Historical Roots of Russian Fairy Tales*:

> Although the customs of millennia are disregarded, the plot of the story still reflects the spirit of those laws and describes every love thwarted and forbidden by law, convention or social disparity. That is why it has been possible, from prehistory to the present, to preserve, not as a fixed formula but as a flowing element, the sensuality so often underlying this love, evident in the ecstasy and frenzy of mysterious nocturnal embraces.

The sensual aspect of love is palpable in Máire Ruiséal's version of the story and, as with the storytelling of Peig Sayers, there is an openness of mind in it about human nature, which one might, perhaps, not expect from the general stereotype of the female storyteller as a pillar of society:

> They entered a fine court. He spoke to her then: 'Wisha, now tell me then,' says he, 'which would you prefer, for me to be a goat at night and a man by day or a man by day and a goat at night?' 'Oh to be sure,' says she, 'I prefer nocturnal company – for you to be a man at night and a goat by day.' And that's the way it was. ('The Story of the White Kid Goat', from the telling of Máire Ruiséal, NFC 243: 162)

I noticed as I visited the Department of Folklore that my interests had changed. Recently I have become more drawn to little bits of local lore, innocent wee stories about people. A certain Sítheach from Baile Eaglaise describing how many houses fell in every townland during the Great Famine. Peats Dhónaill (Ó Cíobháin) from Muiríoch talking about fishing or about Tomás na bPúcaí, a relation of mine. He had a story about Tomás and I'm afraid I have to contradict it. Three young women were pregnant in the village of Leataoibh Meanach. Tomás na bPúcaí had second sight and he said the village would be under a great pall of loss, but he wouldn't say which of the young women would be taken away. As it happened, it was the woman he was most closely related to, the wife of his sister's son. She died of the puerperal mania bringing a daughter into the world and, says Peats Dhónaill, 'She died shortly afterwards and the daughter died as well' (from the telling of Peats Dhónail (Ó Cíobháin), NFC). Well, the daughter didn't die. She was my grandmother and if she hadn't lived I wouldn't be here now.

Another story belonging to my own people I used as an introduction to my last volume, *Cead Aighnis*:

A Person's Three Souls

I was in bed, asleep, down in Baile Móir, when something brought Eoghainín Finton outside, and he saw me emerging from the house.

He called his wife, Léan Ní Chearna. 'Your soul from the devil, Léan,' says he, 'Seán has had a stroke or something! Look at him there by the side of the house. Go out,' says he, 'and call on him.' But he saw me turning again and going back into the house – Léan never called on me. They were telling me this the following day and I wouldn't believe Eoghainín, except that Léan was saying it too. I told him I hadn't left the bed since the time I got into it until the morning, and that I had slept soundly. 'Such things exist,' says Léan, 'and I remembered it. Had I called on him that time,' says Léan, 'he'd be stuck there forever.'

But I've always heard the person to have three parts. There's the soul of the breath, the soul of feeling and the eternal soul. The eternal soul will stay in you until you die. I don't know was it the soul of breath or the soul of feeling in me that was outside while I was asleep, that I don't know. (From the telling of Seán Uí Chíobháin, NFC 965: 63)

But to return to the story at the beginning of my talk, about 'fetters of silk on the sheep of Cathair', I was at the Department of Folklore the other day and happened to discover some more information about it. I always understood it to be a mythological event. It was a remarkable example, or so I thought, of the poetical mind of the people and of the strong imagination always associated with the people of Corca Dhuibhne. I never imagined it to have any historical basis, but it has. The *Lady Nelson* was a big sailing ship that was wrecked on the Skellig, and she was laden with pipes of wine and silk. It was after this ship was wrecked that they built the lighthouse on Skellig:

It was a foggy night and the captain was saying that they were three leagues from land. Some of the crew were of another mind and right they were, because it wasn't long before the ship hit the Skellig. They all drowned except three of them who got up on some floating wood. Two or three days of fog and rain went by and the pipes of wine were washing up on land. Boats were out looking for them. Ventry Harbour and Cathair an Treantaigh were full of boats. There was a man called Scanlon who had a boat and a crew in the bay looking for the wine, when they saw the flotsam and jetsam and the men atop. There were only two left when they reached them. A little while before, the third man had fallen into the water, heavy with sleep. They took the two survivors on board. No more were saved. Later, the two men sent Scanlon and his crew a mast and two sails out of gratitude.

I hope I have thrown some light on the importance that Irish folklore holds for me, and on the importance of the Folklore Commission's collection. I believe folklore works on two levels, firstly on the level of Irish in which I am reminded of the compactness of the everyday language I heard as a child from mouth to mouth in the farmyards. It also works on the level of the imagination when the motifs of the stories – and even the bits of lore scattered throughout the manuscripts – create wonderful images with which one can play, throwing them up in the air and catching them again. And of course that play is one of the most necessary ingredients when it comes to creative writing.

The essence of my lecture has to do with beings not alive, and things that aren't there. Well, until recently I could have sworn that this was the name of a section in the general catalogue of the Department of Folklore in Ireland, a catalogue created by one of the founders of the Department, the collector Seán Ó Súilleabháin. Alas, when I went looking for it – for the purposes of this talk – I couldn't find it. I searched and searched, but there wasn't a trace of it, so maybe there is good reason to believe that it was never there in the first place and I had only dreamt it all along.

I would like to leave the last word to Gearóid Ó Crualaoich from *The Book of the Cailleach: Stories of the Wise-Woman Healer*, a section from the chapter 'Tradition and Theory', because Gearóid says what I am trying to convey in this lecture:

The texts of the oral narrative presented in this book and the commentaries offered with them bear witness, hopefully, to the way that tradition material, frequently seen as outmoded, naïve, parochially-bound, can constitute a rich imaginative resource for our own times and our own circumstances in a world where the local and the global are intermeshing at an increased rate for greater numbers and in ways not previously imagined.

We have a fantastic resource in the oral tradition of Ireland, taken here from the Department's manuscripts and from the ordinary speech of storytellers such as Bab Feirtéar and her two CDs, issued in 2006, which are enjoying such a success that I believe they have sold out twice.

I am not particularly interested in bringing linguistic ranges or literary exemplars into Irish *per se*, though I will consult science, physics or chemistry dictionaries if, for example, I need to describe natural phenomena such as the Northern Lights, which I once saw on a trip to Fairbanks, Alaska. What I would like to do above everything else is to use the natural resources of the language, resources not previously found in the poetry, in any language. That's why I go rummaging in the Department of Folklore and with the help of gods and demons, of beings not alive and things that don't exist, I'll be doing it as long as I am around.

HERE ENDS THE LECTURE. THANKS BE TO GOD.

A transcript of a lecture given in University College Dublin in October 2003.

BIOGRAPHICAL NOTE

Born in Lancashire in 1952 to Irish parents, Nuala Ní Dhomhnaill was brought up in the Dingle Gaeltacht and in Nenagh, County Tipperary, and was educated at University College Cork. Her collections of poetry include *An Dealg Droighin* (1981), *Féar Suaithinseach* (1984), *Rogha Dánta/Selected Poems* (1986, 1988, 1990), *Pharaoh's Daughter* (1990), *Feis* (1991), *The Astrakhan Cloak* (1992), *Spíonáin is Róiseanna* (1993), *In the Heart of Europe: Poems for Bosnia* (1998), *Cead Aighnis* (2000) and *The Fifty Minute Mermaid* (2007). Her *Selected Essays* were published in 2005. She received Duais Sheáin Uí Ríordáin in 1982, 1984 and 1990, Duais Na Chomhairle Ealaíne um Filíochta in 1985 and 1988, Gradam an Oireachtais (1984), the Irish American Foundation O'Shaughnessy Award for Poetry (1988), and the American Ireland Fund Literature Prize (1991). Nuala Ní Dhomhnaill lives in Dublin, is a member of Aosdána, and was Ireland Professor of Poetry 2001–4.

ACKNOWLEDGEMENTS

The author and the publisher gratefully acknowledge the following for permission to reprint copyrighted material. Every effort has been made to seek copyright clearance on referenced text. If there are any omissions, UCD Press will be pleased to insert the appropriate acknowledgement in any subsequent printing or editions.

Nuala Ní Dhomhnaill: 'The Race', translated by Derek Mahon, from *Pharaoh's Daughter* (The Gallery Press, 1990), 'Closure' and 'Plutonium', translated by Eiléan Ní Chuilleanáin, and 'Eithne the Hun', translated by Medbh McGuckian, from *The Water Horse* (The Gallery Press, 1999). All reproduced by kind permission of The Gallery Press. 'Donnacha Di's Testimony', 'Feeding a Child', 'The Mermaid' and 'Mór Anguished', translated by Michael Hartnett, from *Selected Poems/Rogha Dánta* (Raven Arts Press, 1988). Reproduced by kind permission of New Island. 'Primavera', translated by Caoimhín Mac Giolla Léith, reproduced by his kind permission

BIBLIOGRAPHY

Osborn Bergin, 'Unpublished Irish Poems. X: Art versus Nature', *Studies: An Irish Quarterly Review*, Vol. 9, No. 34 (Jun., 1920), pp. 261–3.

Italo Calvino: *Italian Folktales* (Penguin Classics, 2000).

Yunus Emre: 'Aşkın Aldı Benden Beni'/'Your Love Has Wrested Me Away from Me', from *Yunus Emre and His Mystical Poetry*, translated by Talat Sait Halman (Indiana University Press, 1991).

Kenneth Jackson: *A Celtic Miscellany* (Penguin Books, 1971).

Nicholas Kearney: *Transactions of the Ossianic Society for the Year 1854*, volume II (Ossianic Society, 1855).

Seán Mac Airt: *Leabhar Branach: The Book of the O'Byrnes* (The Dublin Institute for Advanced Studies, 1944).

NFC: National Folklore Department, University College Dublin.

Nuala Ní Dhomhnaill: 'Eithne Uathach' and 'Plútóiniam', from *Cead Aighnis* (An Sagart, 1998); 'An Mhaighdean Mhara', 'Mór Cráite' and 'Teist Dhonncha Dí ar Mhór', from *An Dealg Droighin* (Mercier, 1981); 'Ag Cothú Linbh' and 'An Rás', from *Féar Suaithinseach* (An Sagart, 1984); 'Clabhsúr' and 'Primavera', from *Feis* (An Sagart, 1991); 'The Race', translated by Derek Mahon, from *Pharaoh's Daughter* (The Gallery Press, 1990); 'Donnacha Dí's Testimony', 'Feeding a Child', 'The Mermaid' and 'Mór Anguished', translated by Michael Hartnett, from *Selected Poems/Rogha Dánta* (Raven Arts Press, 1988); 'Closure' and 'Plutonium', translated by Eiléan Ní Chuilleanáin, and 'Eithne the Hun', translated by Medbh McGuckian, from *The Water Horse* (The Gallery Press, 1999).

Breandán Ó Buachalla: *Nua-Dhuanaire II* (The Dublin Institute for Advanced Studies, 1976).

Gearóid Ó Crualoich: *The Book of the Cailleach: Stories of the Wise Woman Healer* (Cork University Press, 2006).

Cecile O'Rahilly (ed.): Táin Bó *Cúalnge from the Book of Leinster* (Dublin Institute for Advanced Studies, 1967).

Seán Ó Tuama: *Caoineadh Airt Uí Laoghaire* (An Clóchomhar Tta, 1961).

RBÉ: Roinn Bhéaloideas Éireann / National Folklore Department, University College Dublin.

Mevlana Djellal a-Din Rumi: 'Come, come, whoever you are', from *Sufi Poems: A Mystic Collection from Some Spiritual Poets* (Mesut Sezer, 2015).

Jonathan Swift: 'O Rourke's Ructions', from *Collected Poems of Jonathan Swift*, 2 volumes, edited by Joseph Horrell (Routledge & Kegan Paul, 1958).

Aşık Veysel: 'Kara Toprak'/'The Black Earth', available at: proz.com/kudoz/turkish_to_english/folklore/873356-dost_dost_diye_nicesine_sarıldım_benim_sadık_yarim_kara_topraktır.html